ARCHIPELAGO OF PROTOCOLS
BY ARISTIDE ANTONAS

ARCHIPELAGO OF PROTOCOLS
BY ARISTIDE ANTONAS

Edited by dpr-barcelona

CONTENTS

Foreword

by

Keller

Easterling

Archipelago of Protocols is a much more unusual document than it may first appear to be. In these pages, Aristide Antonas presents five spatial ideas for Athens—collective roof terraces, outdoor rooms, communal work tables, sectional layers of urban space and networks of vacant shops—but the book is not a monograph of design projects. The ideas deploy all the skills associated with architectural training and practice, but they stake out territory outside the typical practices of the profession. Similarly, while they are designs for urban space, they do not suggest policies for urban planning. Together, the protocols appear to create a small list, but they really call for an act of endlessly listing. They are explicitly authored and represented, yet they are also deliberately designed to relinquish authorship to others over time.

    In the same way that this document is not a monograph, the protocols that are the subject of the book are not fixed, finite things, but instructions for how to make evolving things. Protocols—whether used to describe diplomacy, software, manners or space—establish sequences, routines, or relationships between parts, that unfold over time. Protocols lend a disposition or behavior to an arrangement.

In Athens, the five protocols introduce an object, a volume or a relationship that is positioned to interact with the network of activities and stories around it. Using the analogy to software, the protocols offer architectural structures as well as bits of code that align with and continue to shape the urban operating system. So the protocols offer object forms, but beyond the often inert architectural object, they also introduce active forms. They contact a particular time of day, recognize an urban practice, uncover a historical enterprise or provide linkages that, once activated, become engines of ongoing spatial production.

Protocols that are analogous to software are perhaps also analogous to theatrical scripts. A script offers text like an architect offers object form. But the text is really only a trace of or a clue to the action that the performer chooses to play—the action that is often the main carrier of information. Although the author does not prescribe them, in performance these active forms often even overwhelm the text. The black and white aesthetic regime of the drawings in this book —different from the usual antic cartoons of architectural renderings— is even something like the best plays that rarely impose stage directions. Antonas offers some scripts and stories for the city that are suggestive of activities, then, like a good playwright, he leaves the performance to the city itself.

In many ways there is nothing unusual about urban protocols. Most cities run from fragments of code that establish partial protocols appearing and expiring over time. They rarely follow a master plan that is the official document of spatial arrangements. Powerful forces circulate in any city, often finding loopholes and other techniques for shaping urban policy and welfare to serve private power. Recently, the global financial industry has made urban property into trafficked mortgage products, and the most powerful urban players have been trading in real estate variables that are largely divorced from their spatial reality. Athens received a devastating, if indirect, hit from the recent global financial crisis, one symptom of which are the vacancies that appear in several of the projects that Antonas contemplates.

Perhaps the spectacular failures of the financial collapse offer (to the resourceful or the sly designer) a paradoxical opportunity for an alternative market and another form of collective confidence. Rather than the abstract and bankrupted financial variables of speculation, Aristide Antonas offers tangible spatial variables. As if to say simply that all that is needed is almost already there, the newly enhanced qualities and values of space are the things that are exchanged and traded by ordinary people in possession of their city again.

Architecture culture has sometimes regarded these kinds of proposals to be deliberately marginal, sensitive or temporary— the compensatory gentle activity of the powerless. But what if the dispositions suggested by these protocols, like the disposition of their designer, is more powerful by being less insistent. The components of these spatial arrangements are occasionally ephemeral and indeterminate, but they are, perhaps ironically, indeterminate to be practical. And these time-released forms—these active forms— potentially have a longer presence in the city as an urban practice. Finally, far from marginal this document perharps presents nothing less than an alternative species of form-making as well as an alternative habit of mind about urban space.

In theorizing about disposition, and a cultural tendency to privilege things over process—objects over activities—philosopher Gilbert Ryle often wrote about the importance of not only "knowing that" but also "knowing how." If so, these five Protocols are an exercise in "knowing how" for the city of Athens.

The Diagonal Commonhold

Where an act of common possession is affirmed in a lawful tactic; on the basis of a legal protocol holding land without claims to proprietary ownership is accepted; the protocol operates through online registration and processing; the protocol allows the common possession through a system of individual agreements operated on the web.

Article 1
Concepts of diagonal commonhold and plane
A diagonal commonhold is defined as the de facto form of an act of common possession over a plane or a multitude of planes, for the purposes of common use. A diagonal commonhold does not give rise to any proprietary rights. A plane is defined as the determined space in which is established a diagonal commonhold. A plane is spatially determined at the intersection between horizontal and/or vertical legal ownership, which forms shared space. The diagonal commonhold of a plane in a building block, or a multitude of blocks, renders temporarily dormant the proprietary ownership, or co-ownership, of the particular plane or planes of the specific building block or blocks. A determined plane, for the duration of a diagonal commonhold, institutes a temporary autonomous field of diagonal commonhold, which is established for the purposes of common use.

Article 2
Concept of common use

A common use is defined as the type of use that consists of an openly accessible, not-for-profit, occupation and function, which takes place on a plane or a multitude of planes in a building block. A common use established by diagonal commonhold entails the potential for the horizontal participation of registered members of the commonhold in its administration, determination and function. A common use does not require, or give rise to, any proprietary claims.

Article 3
Formation of a diagonal commonhold

The majority agreement of the owners and possessors of the building block is required to formally confirm the diagonal commonhold. The commonhold is placed under the administration of a diagonal committee as defined by article 5.

Article 4
Merger of diagonal commonholds

A diagonal commonhold, at the time of its institution, or at a later point, can be merged with diagonal commonholds of adjacent building blocks. This merger can be authorized by a majority decision of the registered proprietors of each building block.

Article 5
Concept and responsibility of the diagonal committee

The diagonal committee is composed of five members who are elected by the majority of the community of proprietors of the building block in which a diagonal commonhold is established. The election takes place at the site of diagonal commonhold. The diagonal committee undertakes the responsibility to administer the commonhold, the approved use, and to declare its composition and majority decisions at the site of diagonal commonhold.

Article 6
Merger of diagonal committees

In accordance with article 4, in the case of a merger of adjacent diagonal commonholds, the independent diagonal committees are simultaneously merged and form a single diagonal committee of the multitude. The numerical composition of the joint diagonal committee multiplies accordingly.

Article 7
Responsibilities of the diagonal committee

The diagonal committee undertakes the responsibility for the reconstruction, repair and use of the determined plane in which the diagonal commonhold is constituted. The diagonal committee's responsibility can include the installation of horizontal roof coating, shading support structures and solar cells, on the condition that a civil engineer formally approves them.

Article 8
Site of diagonal commonhold
The construction and publication of a unique, openly accessible site of diagonal commonhold is a prerequisite for the institution of a diagonal commonhold. The site of diagonal commonhold must be formally registered as a non-profit organization of common uses. The institution of each diagonal commonhold, its administrative bodies, the list of its registered general members, and all the decisions and operations it involves must be published at the dedicated archive of each diagonal commonhold of the site of diagonal commonhold.

Article 9
Resolution of disputes
The diagonal committee undertakes to provide a conciliatory platform for the consideration and resolution of any arising disputes between proprietors, or between proprietors and possessors, with regard to the institution and function of a diagonal commonhold. The process shall require the online submission of formal objections at the site of diagonal commonhold, followed by an online voting procedure among its registered proprietor and possessor

members. In the event of a majority decision in favour of the institution of a diagonal commonhold, the confirmation of the diagonal commonhold will be considered temporarily obligatory for the duration of the common use. In the event of an objection to the approved common use by a minority, it is required that, at the end of the common use, the diagonal commonhold be dissolved. Upon the dissolution of the diagonal commonhold the building must be returned to the structural and decorative state in which it was before the establishment of a diagonal commonhold.

Shared Terraces

The first protocol, 'The Diagonal Commonhold', defined by an act of common possession without any propietary rights can be found in this project using the fragmented spaces of a block, which are unified as forming a material continuum through added ladders and light stairs that bridge gaps between different levels of buildings; a simultaneous procedure unifies the fragmented unused common properties to a sole common property continuum. This unity of blocks is shown by the construction of light canopies over the terraces; the canopies support grids for shading and light photovoltaic membranes and produce electricity for the inhabitants of the block.

19   Shared Terraces

Shared Terraces

21   Shared Terraces

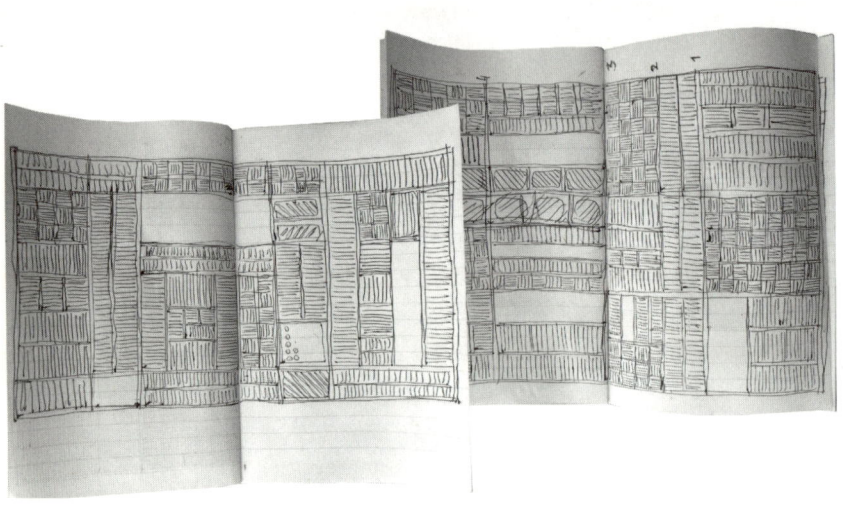

The first protocol gives the legislative background for the Shared Terraces project, it is a legislative unification of blocks and power production on terraces, where the intersection between horizontal and/or vertical legal ownership forms shared space. In Athens the terraces form a forgotten landscape and a system of *terrains vagues*.

23   Shared Terraces

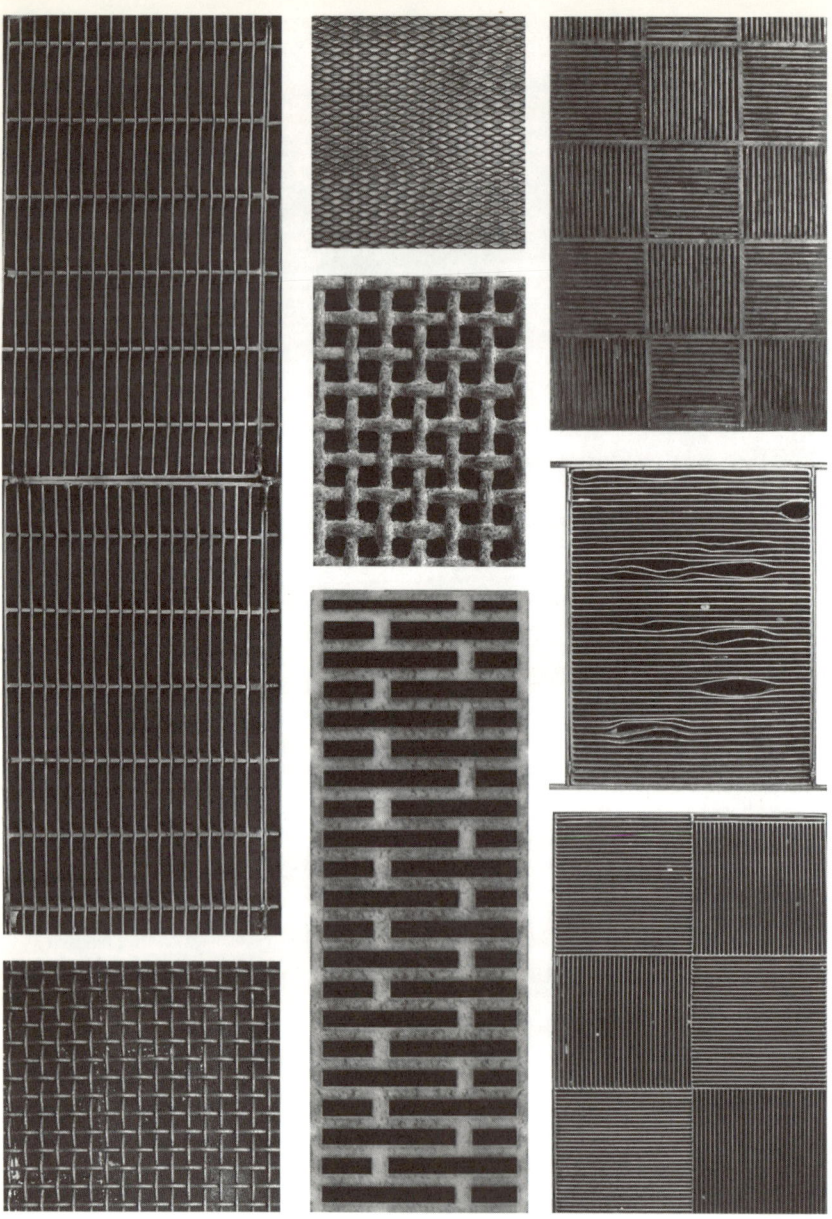

24   Shared Terraces

25   Shared Terraces

Shared Terraces

27   Shared Terraces

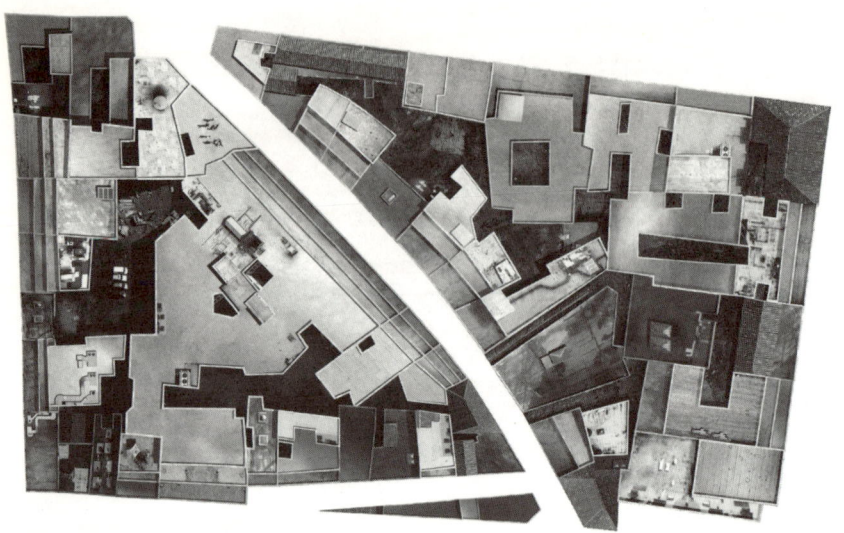

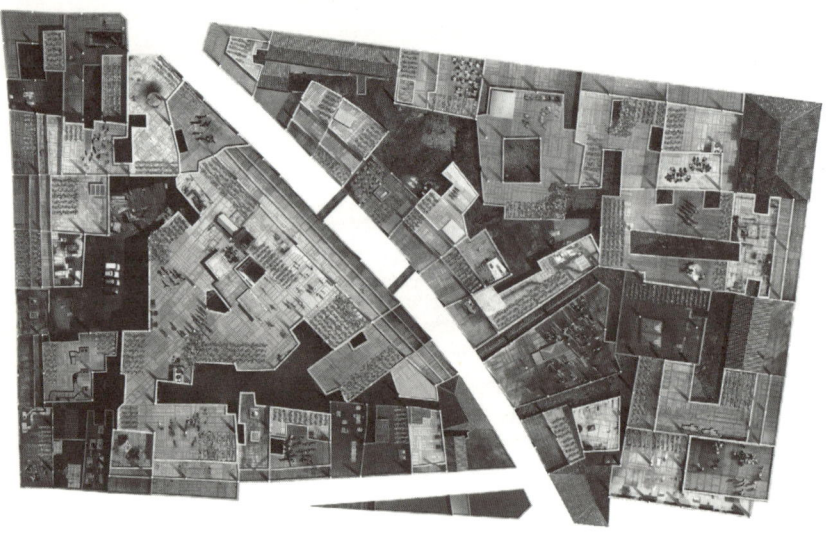

28   Shared Terraces

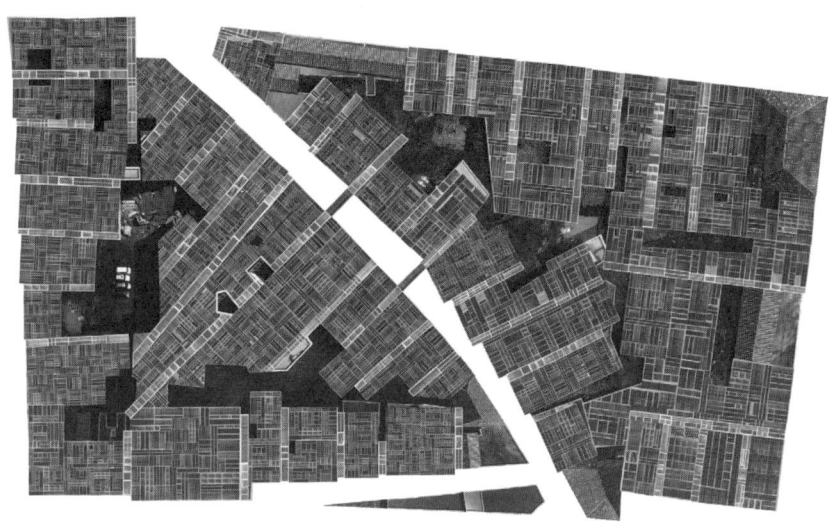

29   Shared Terraces

Shared Terraces

31   Shared Terraces

33   Shared Terraces

A lawful tactic installs a form of holding land without claims of proprietary ownership; this is operated on the basis of a commonly agreed text
that one can sign on the web through online registration and processing;
it allows the common use of a space.

Roof Playgrounds

On Article 4, the 1st Protocol refers to a merger of diagonal common-holds, which so far can be defined by the installation of a large number of ladders, slides and horizontal bars that are placed in some Athenian adjacent center blocks. The additional metallic objects are going to be created by artisans working in Athens without general or detailed architectonic plans: the execution description for the construction would be the only design; an indication of the connection points and the type of each connection is what replaces here the architectural drawings. The program could conclude by bridging different city blocks through the use of suspension bridges between them.

39   Roof Playgrounds

Repeatability, hypnotic in itself, is usually founded by cyclical durations. The depth of human desires, is often based on installations of repetitions. This hypnotic potential is projected here on some playful landscape, which already exists in the roofs of Athens. This invisible and diverse roof landscape of the city would then be a shared urban space and an area of particular motion.

41   Roof Playgrounds

43   Roof Playgrounds

44   Roof Playgrounds

The Invisible Council

Where an internet site forms the plateau of an affirmative common power of holding over "indeterminate spaces"; "indetermination" establishes common use functions without proprietary rights.

The structure of the Internet site allows decisions for common strategies through chosen algorithms. Registration, processing and distributing are the steps one has to follow in order to operate in this frame.

Article 1
Concept of an Indeterminate Space

An Indeterminate Space is defined as the public or private space that remains unoccupied and not exploited in any manner, for a continuous period of five years.

Article 2
Concept of Diagonal Commonhold

A space characterized as an Indeterminate Space can be subjected to a Diagonal Commonhold for the purposes of common use by a temporary de facto occupation that renders any existent proprietary status dormant. A Diagonal Commonhold does not give rise to any proprietary rights.

Article 3
Concept of Common Use

A Common Use is defined as the type of use that consists of an openly accessible, not-for-profit, occupation and function, which takes place on an

Indeterminate Space. A common use established by Diagonal Commonhold entails the potential for the horizontal participation of registered members of the Commonhold in its administration, determination and function. A Common Use does not require, or gives rise to, any proprietary claims.

Article 4
Validity and Terms of a Diagonal Commonhold
The state of a temporary Diagonal Commonhold over an Indeterminate Space becomes valid when after the end of a continuous period of five years of indeterminacy, members of the local neighborhood who have formed an Invisible Neighborhood (as established by Article 5) take physical possession of it. The possession of the specific space is characterized as temporarily legal, if the following terms are satisfied: (a) the possession takes place and is held without violence; (b) the possession is realized and maintained without approval, agreement or intervention by the proprietary holder or holders; (c) the occupied Indeterminate Space is subjected to a Diagonal Commonhold; and (d) the acts of possession, occupation and administration are declared and processed at the Site of Diagonal Commonhold.

Article 5
Constitution of the Invisible Council and the Invisible Neighborhood

On the first day of the de facto possession by occupation of an Indeterminate Space, an Invisible Council, comprised of five registered members of the local Neighborhood, must be elected and declared at the Site of Diagonal Commonhold. The Invisible Council must be elected by a majority voting procedure at the Site of Diagonal Commonhold by an electorate body of registered members of the local neighborhood. The majority is to be determined from an electorate of a minimum of 50 registered members. The Invisible Council assumes responsibility for the temporary possession, occupation and administration of the approved use or uses in the specified Indeterminate Space. The registered members of the local neighborhood constitute, by registration, the Invisible Neighborhood of the said Diagonal Commonhold. An application for registration and membership can be submitted online at the dedicated archive of the Site of Diagonal Commonhold by any inhabitant within a distance of 500 meters from the declared Indeterminate Space.

Article 6
Obligations and Responsibility
of the Invisible Council
The Invisible Council undertakes the responsibility for the possession, maintainance and administration of the declared as temporarily expropriated Indeterminate Space. The Invisible Council is responsible for the

supervision of the strict character of common use at
the Indeterminate Space, and undertakes the financial
responsibility for the required utility and other
mandatory costs.

Article 7
Declaration of Acts of the Invisible Council
Each act of use, operation, installation of support
equipment and rearrangement of the affected space
for the purposes of the required common infrastructure and provisions, must be declared on the Site
of Diagonal Commonhold.

Open Air Office

Protocol 2 proposes a site where the Internet forms a plateau of an affirmative common power over 'indeterminate spaces'. This indetermination has been overcome with the installation of public tables in a selected area of the city center; the provision of electricity, Wi-Fi, water, table, lamps and stools by a de facto possession and occupation of an indeterminate space in the city center, creating the conditions for people to gather. In this context, the Open Air Office functions more as a question to this direction than as a specific answer.

Open Air Office

54   Open Air Office

The project's strategy, operating in the derelict, emptied city center, proposes small scale transformations of a place related to the urban fabric in mediated ways. The Open Air Office proposed one such urban function that could organize anew abandoned places in the center of the city.

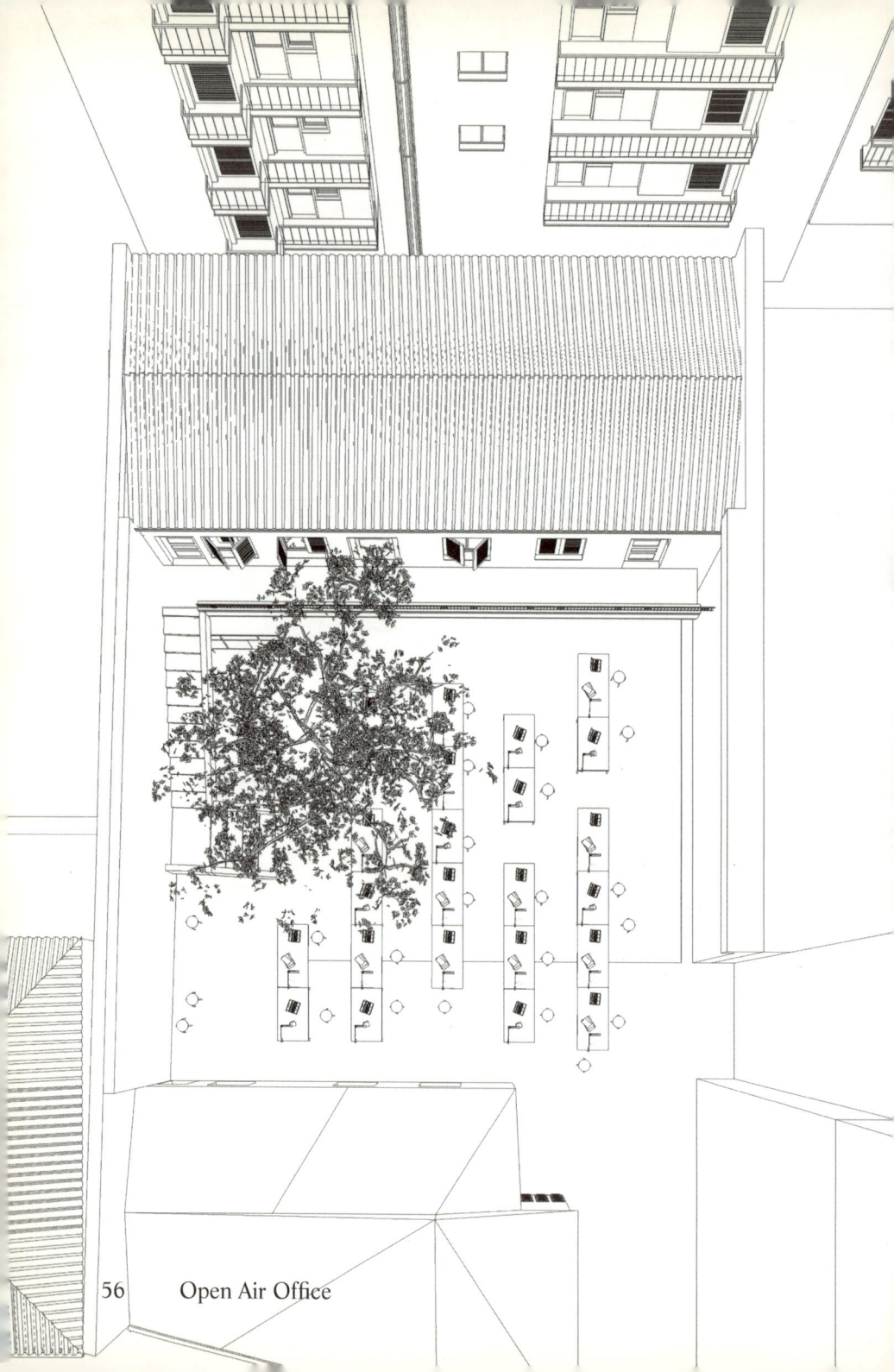

Open Air Office

57   Open Air Office

Open Air Office

60   Open Air Office

61   Open Air Office

Open Air Office

63   Open Air Office

64 Open Air Office

65   Open Air Office

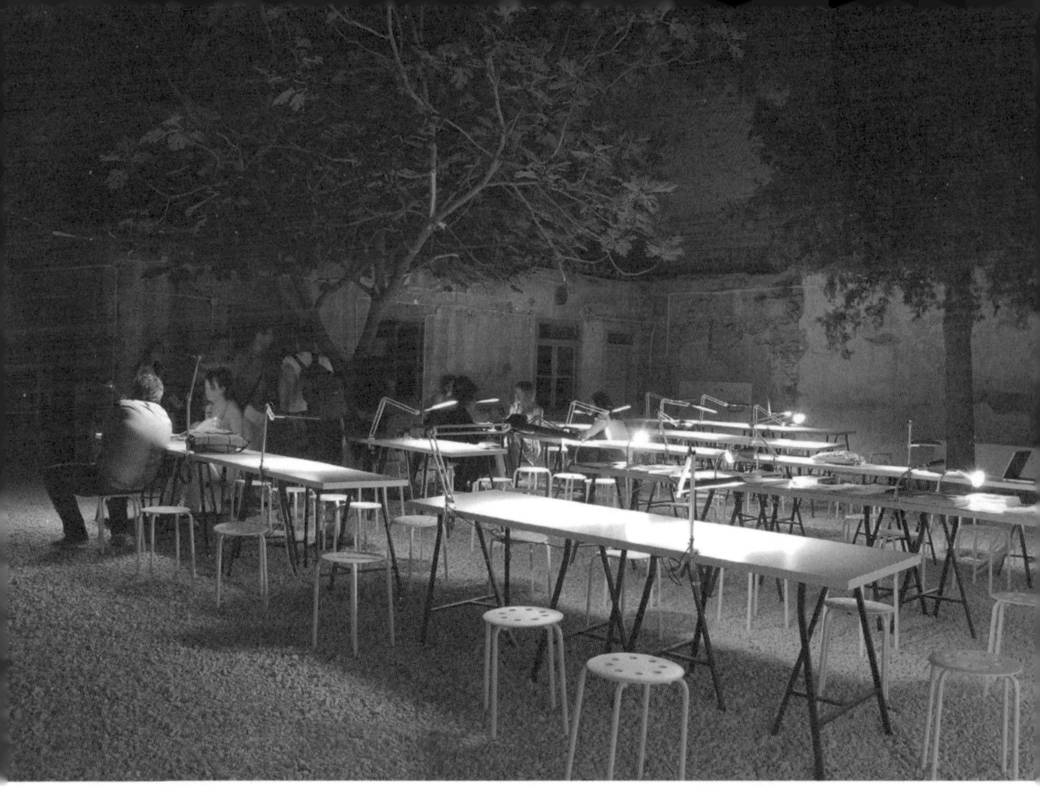

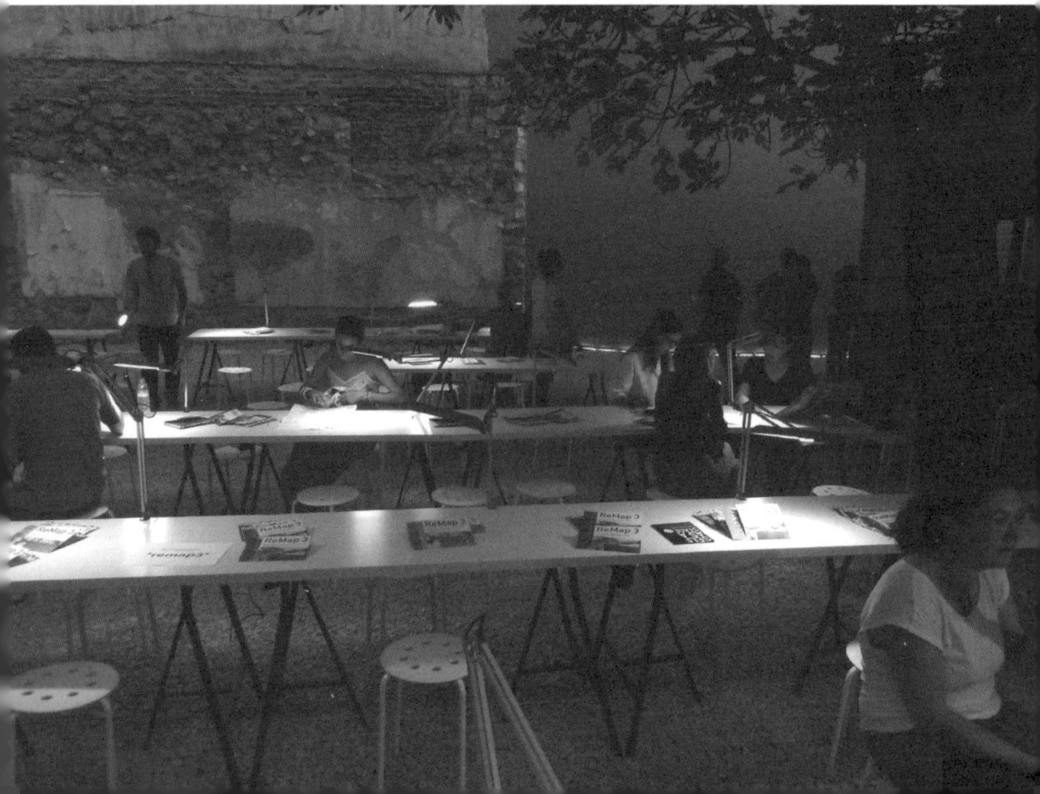

A scenographic installation of a number of tables in a public space transforms the idea of retreat by means of the Internet to a different protocol for gathering. The costless change of the area's lighting can temporarily change its meaning. Architects are called to provide different built readings, not different buildings.

67   Open Air Office

Open Air Office

Radical

Non–use

Where the concept of transitional period of non-use is established; this period allows some protocols to operate; in the same time it facilitates the eventual establishment of the state of radical non-use; the state of radical non-use grounds the common power of expropriation and partial demolitions; expropriation and partial demolitions offer spaces for common uses, without giving rise to proprietary claims but operated by united ex-proprietors or renters.

Article 1
Concepts of Diagonal Commonhold and Plane

A Diagonal Commonhold is defined as the de facto form of an act of common possession over a Plane or a multitude of Planes, for the purposes of common use. A Diagonal Commonhold does not give rise to any proprietary rights. A Plane is defined as the determined space of a building in which is established a Diagonal Commonhold. The Diagonal Commonhold of a Plane in a building, or a multitude of buildings, renders temporarily dormant the proprietary ownership, or co-ownership, over the particular plane or planes of the specific building or buildings. A determined Plane, for the duration of a Diagonal Commonhold, institutes a temporary autonomous field of Diagonal Commonhold, which is established for the purposes of Common Use.

Article 2
Concept of Common Use

A Common Use is defined as the type of use that consists of an openly accessible, not-for-profit, occupation and function, which takes place on a Plane or a multitude of Planes in a building or multitude of buildings. A common use established by Diagonal Commonhold entails the potential for the horizontal participation of registered members of the Commonhold in its administration, determination and function. A Common Use does not require, or give rise to, any proprietary claims.

Article 3
Concept of a Radical State of Non-Use
A Radical State of Non-Use is the de facto state of possession of Planes that remain in a state of non-occupation and non-exploitation, for an uninterrupted term of five years. The state of Radical Non-Use establishes a state of Diagonal Commonhold that does not provide ground for any claim to ownership, or other property rights, over a Plane or parts of a Plane.

Article 4
*Concepts of a Provisional State of Non-Use
and the Transitional period*
A Provisional State of Non-Use of a plane is established exactly one month after the declaration of a state of Non-Use on the Site of Diagonal Common-hold, on the condition that no formal objection is registered by formal notice on the Site of Diagonal

Commonhold, within this period of time, by a person or persons holding legal title or other exclusive proprietary right. The Provisional State of Non-Use of a Plane or part of a Plane is initially established for the duration of a strict two-year provisional term. The term of two years of such Non-Use is defined as the Transitional Period.

Article 5
Suspension of a State of Non-Use during the Transitional Period
The suspension of the Provisional State of Non-Use is realized when an objection is registered by formal notice on the Site of Diagonal Commonhold, by a person or persons holding legal title or other exclusive proprietary right, during the period that begins from the initiation of the Transitional Period and ends one month before the termination of the Transitional Period. The right to formally object is accorded to any natural or legal person that declares and proves the legal ownership of the spatial field within which the plane under Diagonal Commonhold is located. An objection can be registered by notice during the five-year term of Radical Non-Use. The Diagonal Committee as prescribed by Article 7 must consider any formal objection.

Article 6
Operations for the Common Good in a State of Non-Use

The Provisional State of Non-Use, as a temporary state, aims to facilitate the right to develop operations facilitating the common good, as prescribed by Paragraph 1 of the Greek Constitution. Each common use in the name of the common good is defined in accordance to the specific characteristics of each plane upon and through which it operates and on the basis of the declared proposal of the registered members of a Diagonal Committee (as defined by Article 7).

Article 7
Constitution of a Diagonal Committee
During the Transitional Period a five-membered Diagonal Comittee is to be instituted and declared on the Site of Diagonal Commonhold. The Diagonal Committee is authorised to: (a) decide by its majority on the proposed use; (b) administer the applied operation or operations for the purposes of the proposed use; (c) supervise the conformity to the approved use; (d) ensure the safety of the plane over which it operates; and (e) administer the examination and resolution of any submitted objections.

Article 8
Letting a plane under a Diagonal Commonhold
The Diagonal Committee can let, on gratuitous rent, a characterized as a non-used plane or a part of it, upon the application of one or more registered members of the Diagonal Commonhold. The act of letting is

conditioned by the following terms: (a) the duration of
the letting is limited to a term ranging from a minimum
of six months to a maximum of twelve months. The term
can be extended, on a discretionary basis, following
an extension application to the Diagonal Committee.
The term can be annuled during its agreed operation
in the case of a suspension as prescribed by article 5;
(b) The purpose of the letting on gratuitous rent is to
serve the purpose of the operation of a common use
over the plane or part of it; (c) the supervision of the
legality, operative function and administration of
a let plane, or a part of it, remains at all times under
the responsibility of the Diagonal Committee.

Article 9
Public declaration of works and common uses
The Diagonal Committee is required to declare the
planned and executed works on the plane and to submit
an annual report at the Site of Diagonal Commonhold,
and seek its majority approval by the registered
members to the Commonhold.

Article 10
*Planning for the expropriation and reconstruction
of a plane during the transitional period*
During the Transitional Period of a Provisional
State of Non-Use, apart from the approved temporary
uses and acts of letting, the Diagonal Committee is
permitted to plan for and execute the safe demolition

of minor parts of a building, or multitude of buildings, on the plane or planes in question. Planning for the construction and the installation of light scafolding structures that organize the placement of useable containers is permitted under the strict responsibility of the Diagonal Committee. Any demolition and/ or construction and installation must be executed in such manner so that in the event of dissolution of the Commonhold, or suspension due to an objection or state intervention, the plane in question can be returned to the state it were prior to the establishment of the Diagonal Commonhold.

Article 11
The Radical State of Non-Use and the power of expropriation and commonhold

At the expiration of the Transitional Period, without any disruption or suspension, the Provisional State of Non-Use becomes definitive and is characterised as a Radical State of Non-Use. The plane in question is rendered expropriated against a person or persons holding proprietary title or other exclusive proprietary interest. The Diagonal Commonhold remains, at all times, without any claim to ownership or property rights. During the state of Radical Non-Use further acts of demolition, reconstruction and rearrangement of the spatial field or parts of it in question are permitted. In particular, demolitions during the state of Radical Non-Use are required to comply to the principle of potential reversibility to the state prior to the establishment of the Diagonal Commonhold.

Article 12
Claims and Compensation

The definitive Diagonal Commonhold during a State of Radical Non-Use is valid against all, and all proprietary rights by persons concerned are transformed to compensation rights if the proprietors consent to the permanent expropriation of their property. Such compensation claims are to be adjudicated in a conciliatory process according to the principles of the law on unjust enrichment (Article 904 Civil Code). Compensation is payable in kind by the provision of a sufficient number of containers, enabling the claimant to participate in vertical or horizontal commonholding, as determined fairly by the Diagonal Committee and without disturbing the state of Diagonal Commonhold. In the event of valid objections by the concerned, non-consenting, proprietor or proprietors, the specific plane which affects the concerned property must be returned to the state in which it was prior to the establishment of the Diagonal Commonhold within a period of six months from the date of the registration of the objection on the Site of Diagonal Commonhold.

Weak Monumental Square

The third protocol institutes the concept of radical non-use and under certain conditions it can allows demolition's, expropriations and construction of light scaffolding structures in specific semi abandoned parts of the city. The Weak Monumental Square is an example about the possibility of turning this possibility to a unimagined scale.

A dense field of an unused infrastructure offers some of its enclosed spaces to a different public sphere that could be under construction. A strategic decision or redistribution of these empty spaces could rebuild anew a different attitude to the modern ruins that host the city. They can be reused again through different architectures; the intervention of the private sector, which is anyway destroyed, could be a public task. Architecture could have a role to re-elaborate the public sphere as a new, different urban scene.

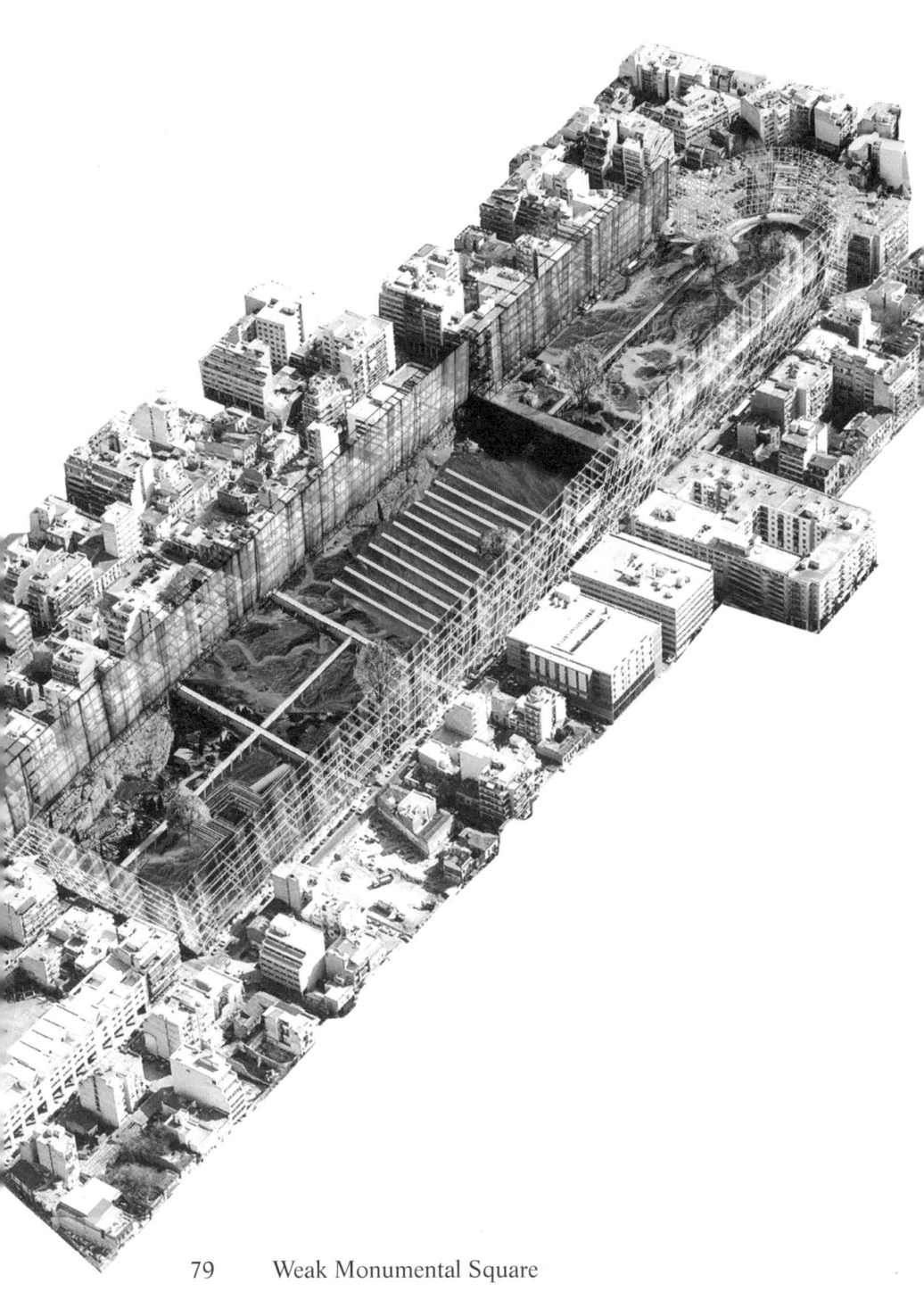

79 Weak Monumental Square

The construction of a weak monument is a memorial of the private properties expropriated for an immense excavation field at the city center.

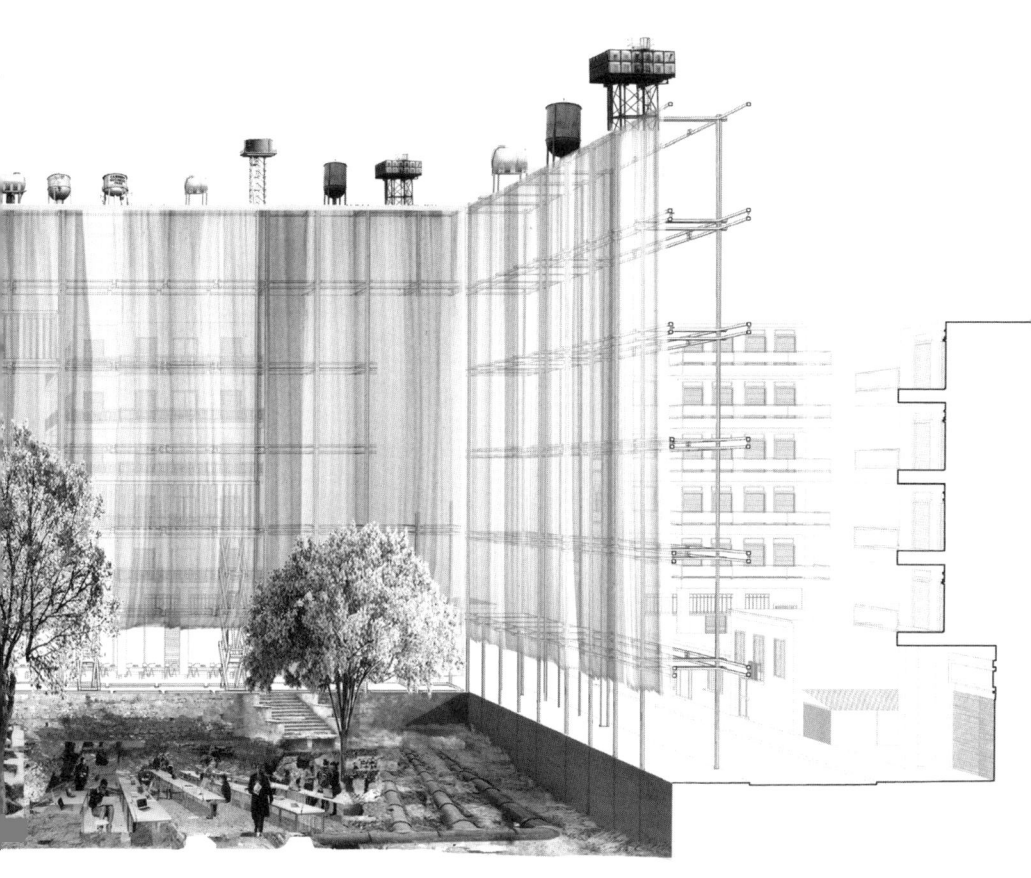

81   Weak Monumental Square

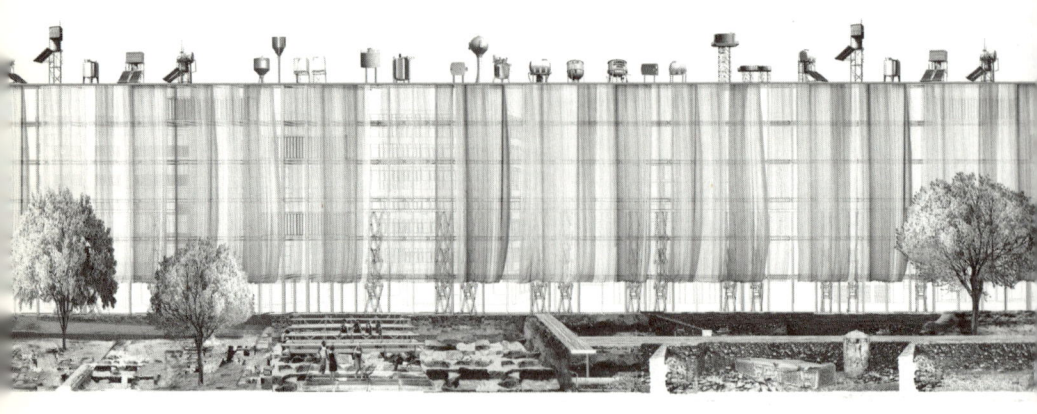

83   Weak Monumental Square

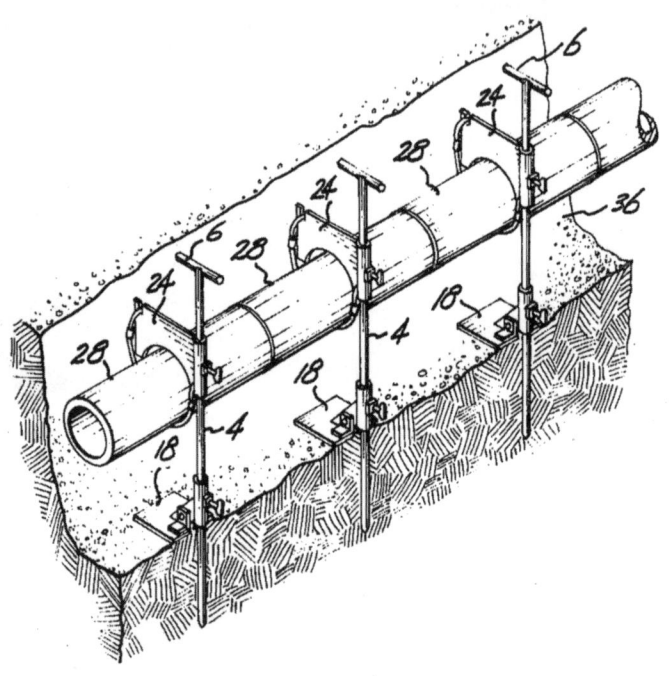

Rhizome of Non—Proprietary Uses

Where non-used private commercial spaces are programmed as an expanding rhizome of planes, allowing
non-proprietary and non-profit common uses.

Article 1
Concepts of diagonal commonhold and plane
A diagonal commonhold is defined as the de
facto form of an act of common possession over a
plane or a multitude of planes, for the purposes of
common use. A diagonal commonhold does not give
rise to any proprietary rights. A plane is defined as
the determined space in which is established a diagonal
commonhold. The diagonal commonhold of a plane
in a private commercial space, or a multitude of private
commercial spaces, renders temporarilly dormant
the proprietary ownership, or co-ownership, of the
particular private commercial space or multitude
of spaces. A determined plane, for the duration of
a diagonal commonhold, institutes a temporary
autonomous field of diagonal commonhold, which
is established for the purposes of common use.

Article 2
Concept of common use
A common use is defined as the type of use that
consists of an openly accessible, not-for-profit,
occupation and function, which takes place on a plane
or a multitude of planes in a private commercial space
or multitude of spaces. A common use established by

diagonal commonhold entails the potential for the horizontal participation of registered members of the commonhold in its administration, determination and function. A common use does not require, or give rise to, any proprietary claims.

Article 3
Concept of a State of Radical Non-Use
A State of Radical Non-Use is the de facto state of possession of Planes that remain in a state of non-occupation and non-exploitation, for an uninterrupted term of five years. The state of Radical Non-Use establishes a state of Diagonal Commonhold that does not provide ground for any claim to ownership, or other property rights, over a Plane or parts of a Plane.

Article 4
Validation and duration of a Provisional State of Non-Use
An initial, Provisional State of Non-Use, when declared over a Plane, is valid upon the expiration of a term of one month from its registered declaration at the Site of Diagonal Commonhold, on the condition that during this term there has been no formal registered objection, by a person or persons holding proprietary ownership or other exclusive proprietary right. At the expiration of the initial one-month period since the required declaration, the state of Diagonal Commonhold, as a result of temporary non-use,

becomes temporarily valid for a term of five years, unless or until a formal objection to it is raised.

Article 5
Expiration of Provisional State of Non-Use
Upon the expiration of the five-year period of an uninterrupted State of Provisional Non-Use of private commercial spaces, whether adjacent, or not, within the range of neighbouring blocks, the Provisional State of Non-Use is declared as a State of Radical Non-Use. In a State of Radical Non-Use an indefinite state of Diagonal Commonhold is established over the relevant Plane or Planes. Upon such a declaration the unification of Planes, where relevant, is permitted under the supervision and administration of a specially formed Rhizomatic Council (as defined by Article 6). For the duration of the Diagonal Commonhold any proprietary ownership or other exclusive proprietary right, over the Plane or Planes, is rendered dormant.

Article 6
Authorization of the Rhizomatic Council
The Rhizomatic Council is to be composed of five registered members of the formed Diagonal Commonhold and must be constituted at the time of the establishment of the Diagonal Commonhold. The Rhizomatic Council undertakes the administrative responsibility over the relevant Plane or Planes, with its sole aim being the approval and supervision of

common, not-for-profit, uses that are to take place
in the single or unified private commercial Plane
or Planes, which are declared as being under a state
of temporary or radical non-use.

Article 7
Approval of Uses and Lettings
The Rhizomatic Council is authorized to approve
the proposed uses over the Plane or unified Planes in
question by applicant private persons or groups, by
a majority voting procedure, which is to take place at
the Site of Diagonal Commonhold. All proposed uses
are to be authorized under a short letting of a strict
term that can range from one hour to one year, in
conjunction with the consideration of a proposed use
by the Rhizomatic Council.

Article 8
Supervision of Commonhold and Letting
The Rhizomatic Council is required to oversee
the common, non-proprietary and not-for-profit
character and operation of the declared Diagonal
Commonhold over a Plane or Planes, under a State
of Radical Non-Use, throughout the duration of each
short letting. The renter is required to compensate
the Rhizomatic Council for any damage, other than
fair wear and tear, and for any non-authorized
alteration applied to the Plane in question, that occur
during the agreed short letting term.

Article 9

Registration of Objections and Resolution of Disputes

In the event of a registered objection by a legal proprietor on the dedicated archive of the Site of Diagonal Commonhold, the Rhizomatic Council is required to inform the legal proprietor or proprietors in question of: (a) the supervision and guarantee of the operative use on the Plane or Planes in question; (b) the clean and safe state and supervision of the Plane or Planes in question; and (c) the financial compensation to the proprietor by the renter for all utility expenses, council taxes and other mandatory costs. If the proprietor or proprietors, upon the receipt of the information and guarantee by the Rhizomatic Council and the renter, wishes to pursue further the objection process, the Rhizomatic Council is required to declare the cessation of all activity and to dissolve the Diagonal Commonhold over the relevant Plane or Planes and to vacate within a strict period of one year from the day of the formal registration of the objection.

Transformable Vertical Village

In Protocol 4, an expanding rhizome of non proprietary and non profit common uses is proposed. In that sense, the urban congregation of ship containers named "vertical mobile village" is a quick solution for temporary housing responding to the needs of new residential areas in Hymetus, Athens, that responds to the requirements of the protocol. Conceived as a "housing library", where the units that form the ensemble can change place, and where the common use is defined as the type of use that consists of an openly accessible, not-for-profit, occupation and function. Here, the structure is conceived as a high, three dimensional infrastructure grid that can receive ready made elementary homes, hosted in ship containers through an interior solution that allows the units to plug in the village's infrastructure.

95 Transformable Vertical Village

The proposal functions as a strategic obligatory space redistribution that is controlled by the state or the municipality and gives to the landlords some space in this vertical village in return for their ground floor shops or offices that are temporarily expropriated, in order that the city center starts functioning again.

99   Transformable Vertical Village

Transformable Vertical Village

Agglomeration of Empty Shops

Non-used private commercial places located in a system of arcades and their extensions are programmed as the rhizome of a common structure, more or less unified; they depend on the decision of a commonhold. Athens is full of empty spaces where the Agglomeration of Empty Shops projects propose to situate small urban cells to create economic or cultural activities in a linear system of Athenian arcades. The proprietors or the renters of the empty shops decide the nature of the business to be placed at every spot. The unity of the intervention is indicated by the continuity of the arcades. At a second level what has to be secured was the exact opposite: the multiplicity of this fragmentary space has to be again secured and guaranteed as the most important part of the intervention. An inhomogeneous functionality is programmed.

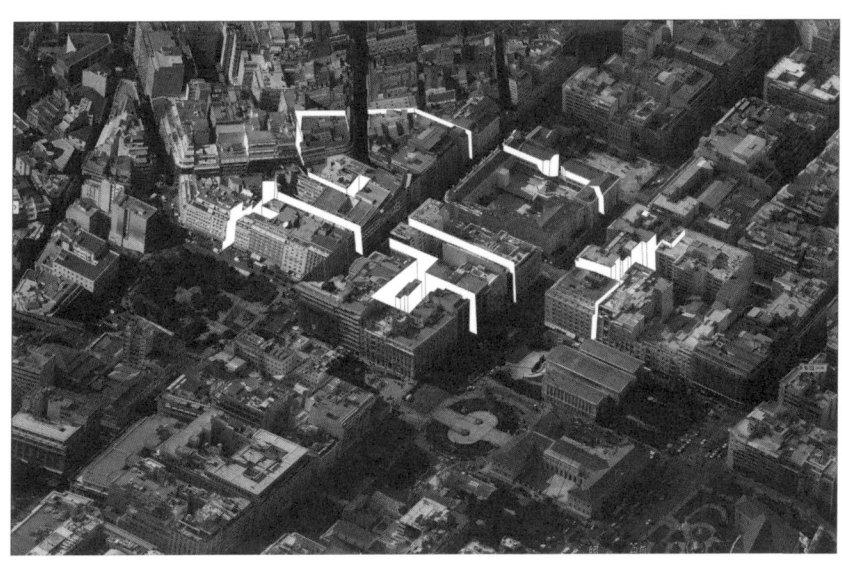

105   Agglomerattion of Empty Shops

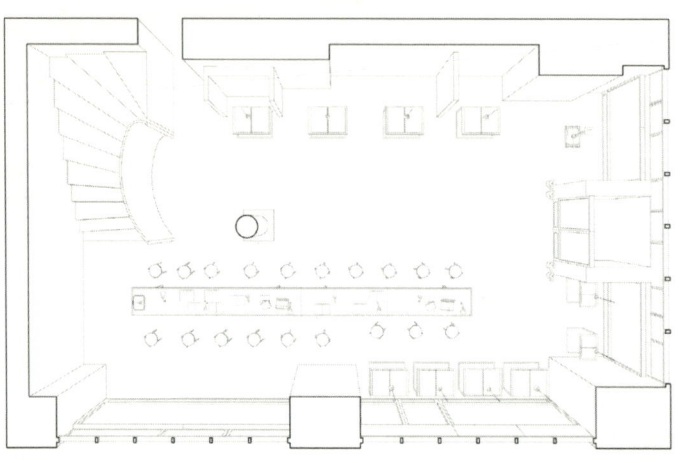

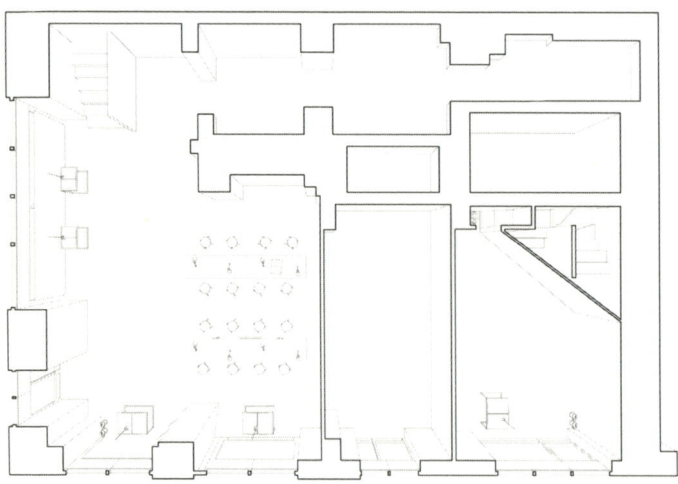

Agglomerattion of Empty Shops

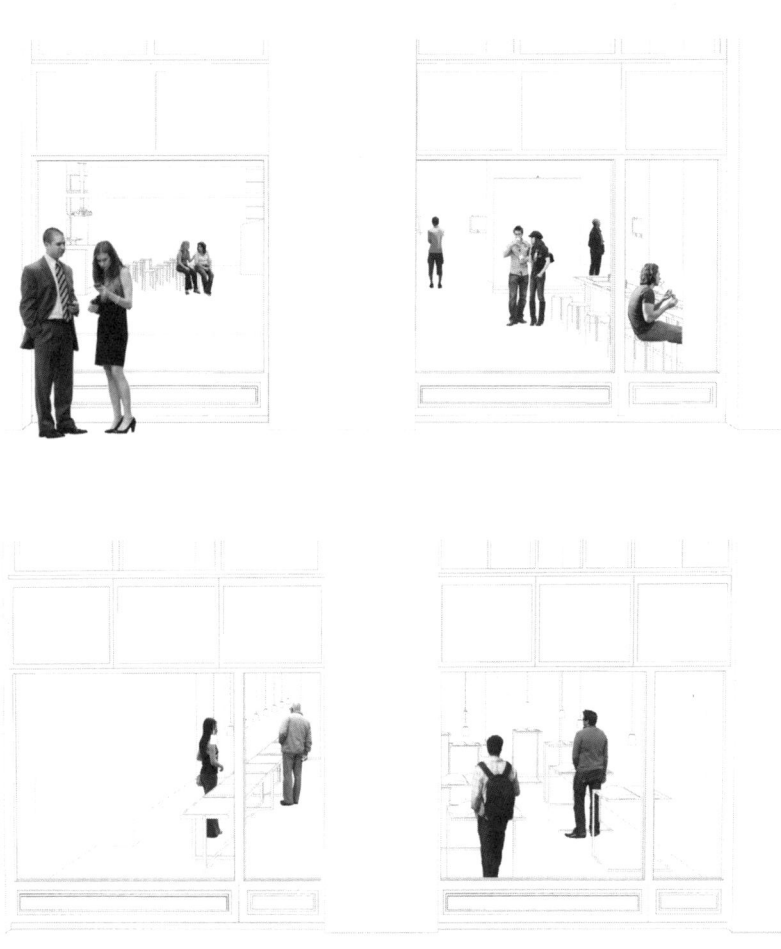

Agglomerattion of Empty Shops

108   Agglomerattion of Empty Shops

The occupation of the empty shops would have to perform at a first level with a singular logic. A space of an open ad-hoc university or a system of discussion rooms or equipped rooms for temporary shows could transform this linear spaces to a different entity.

Agglomerattion of Empty Shops

111   Agglomerattion of Empty Shops

113   Agglomerattion of Empty Shops

Agglomerattion of Empty Shops

115   Agglomerattion of Empty Shops

According to Protocol 4, a new form of commonhold emerges in a commercial space, or a multitude of private commercial spaces. In this project, an unusual urban curating had to firstly define the unity of its intention, organize and colonize the empty space and secondly keep the scale of the small shops in a unified intervention.

117   Agglomerattion of Empty Shops

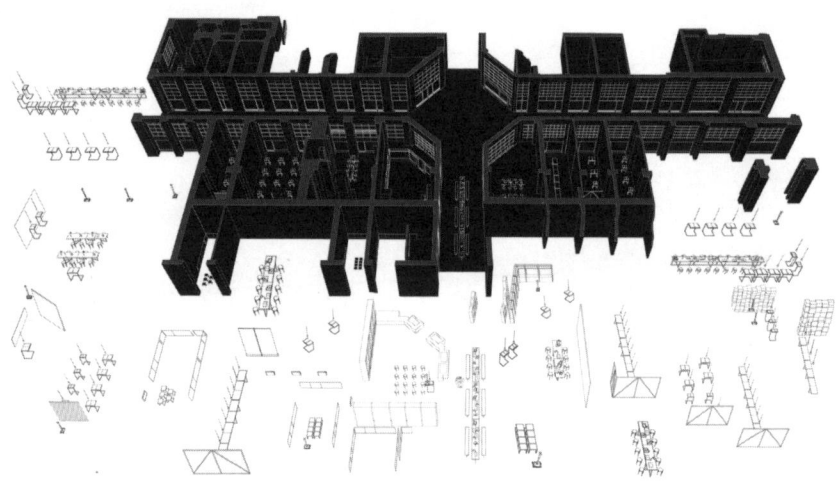

Agglomerattion of Empty Shops

The Parasitic Council

Where a public space can be the plateau for the occupancy of a commonhold in order that it performs multiple parasitic functions of common use without claims to property.

Article 1
Concepts of Diagonal Commonhold and Plane

A Diagonal Commonhold is defined as the de facto form of an act of common possession over a Plane or a multitude of Planes, for the purposes of common use. A Diagonal Commonhold does not give rise to any proprietary rights. A Plane is defined as the determined space of a public space in which is established a Diagonal Commonhold. The Diagonal Commonhold of a Plane in a publicly owned space, renders temporarilly dormant the proprietary ownership, over the particular plane or planes of the specific publicly owned space. A determined Plane, for the duration of a Diagonal Commonhold, institutes a temporary autonomous field of Diagonal Commonhold, which is established for the purposes of Common Use.

Article 2
Concept of Common Use

A Common Use is defined as the type of use that consists of an openly accessible, not-for-profit, occupation and function, which takes place on a Plane or a multitude of Planes in a publicly owned space. A

common use established by Diagonal Commonhold
entails the potential for the horizontal participation of
registered members of the Commonhold in its administration, determination and function. A Common Use
does not require, or give rise to, any proprietary claims.

Article 3
Concept of an Urban Hall
An Urban Hall is defined as the Plane, or part of a
Plane, under public ownership, which is subjected to a
temporary de facto occupation over which a Diagonal
Commonhold is established, that gives rise to non
proprietary rights and is in conformity with the Greek
Constitution.

Article 4
Composition and Authorization
of the Parasitic Council
The Parasitic Council is defined as a council composed of twelve members, which is elected through an
online majority voting procedure at the Site of Diagonal
Commonhold. The authorization of the Parasitic
Council requires a majority vote from an electorate
of registered Diagonal Commonhold members that
satisfies a minimum of three thousand voters.

Article 5
Operational Terms of the Parasitic Council

The authorized Parasitic Council is required to; (a) approve the proposed use or uses according to Article 6; (b) oversee the composition and operation of the Administrative Committee (as prescribed by Articles 7, 8 and 9); and (c) conform to the Terms (as prescribed by Article 8).

Article 6
Approval of proposed Common Uses
Each proposed use must be submitted to the Parasitic Council, by the group of registered residents as members of the Diagonal Commonhold, or by a legal or natural person, at the dedicated archive of the Site of Diagonal Commonhold. It is necessary to attach to the submission of each proposal the following: (a) the exact description of the proposed use; (b) the exact term of the proposed use; and (c) the formal declaration, justification and other supporting documentation of the proposed common use. Each proposal must be subjected to a majority voting procedure, within a month after its submission. The approval, or rejection, of each proposal must be declared at the Site of Diagonal Commonhold.

Article 7
Definition of the Use Committee
The Parasitic Council must approve and authorize the Use Committee, composed of three registered

members of the approved use, who are to be responsible for the organization and safe operation of the approved use for the duration of its term.

Article 8
Terms
The Use Committee must oversee the conformity to the following terms of application and use within the Urban Hall: (a) the common character and operation of the approved use; (b) the clean state of the Urban Hall; (c) the observance of the exact term of the use; (d) the safety and protection of the participants; and (e) the legality of any exercised activity and use.

Article 9
Cessation
In the event of non-conformity to any of the required terms of operation (as defined by Article 8), the de facto Diagonal Commonhold, under the aegis of the Use Committee, can be subjected to a process of cessation by a majority decision of the Parasitic Council. The decision and justification of a cessation must, in each instance, be declared publicly at the Site of the Diagonal Commonhold.

The Trench and the Arcade

The fifth protocol, refers to the public space as a plateau where multiple parasitic functions of common use can happen, after being submitted to the Parasitic Council. In that sense, the Trench and the Arcade project is defined by a re-territorialization performed with new protocols; to see the city of Athens as a function of its perverse ground at the same time idealized for its ruins and undermined as the field of its infrastructure. The various successive layers in the city of Athens correspond to this system of narrative strata. The project tackles the city as a condition that operates with an apparent duality. On one hand, what is stressed is the city's current condition, which classifies Athens as the paradigmatic city in the era of this particular financial moment of the globe. On the other hand, the proposal measures the importance of the city as an urban formation inhabited by traces of both an ancient and a recent past.

127   The Trench and the Arcade

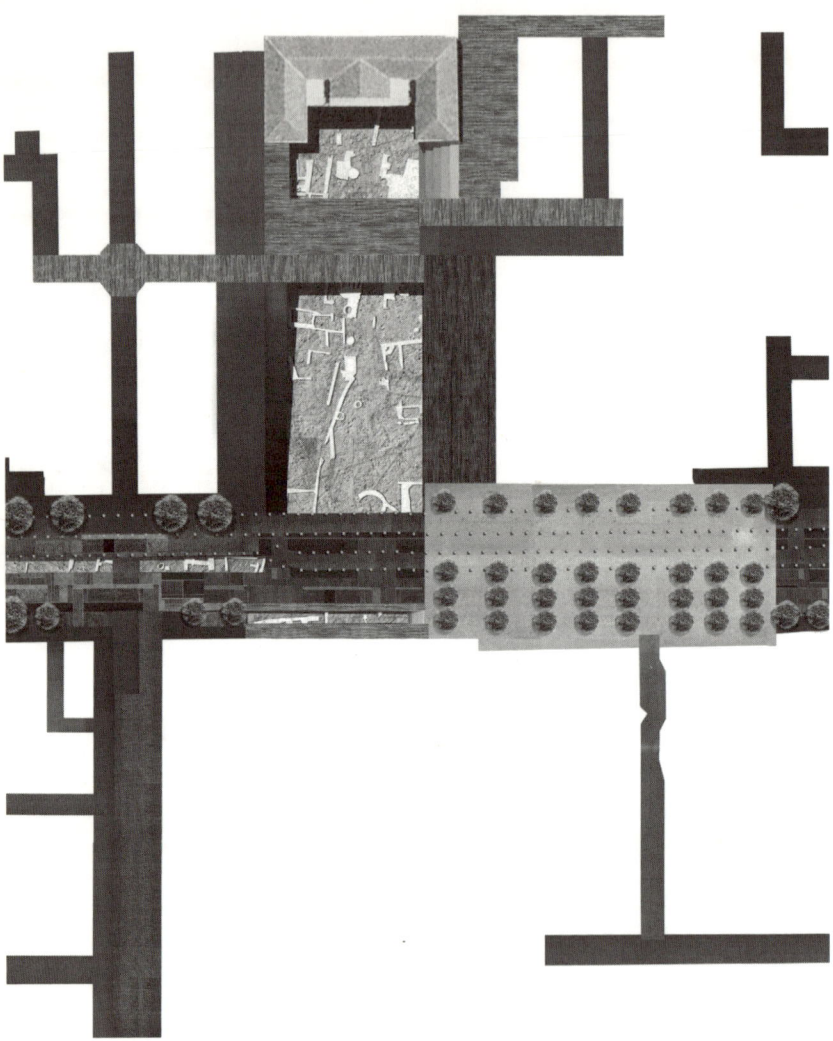

The Trench and the Arcade

129   The Trench and the Arcade

The proposal uncovers, organizes, piles and composes in this particular
moment the fragments of the city's uninterrupted social activity.

The Trench and the Arcade

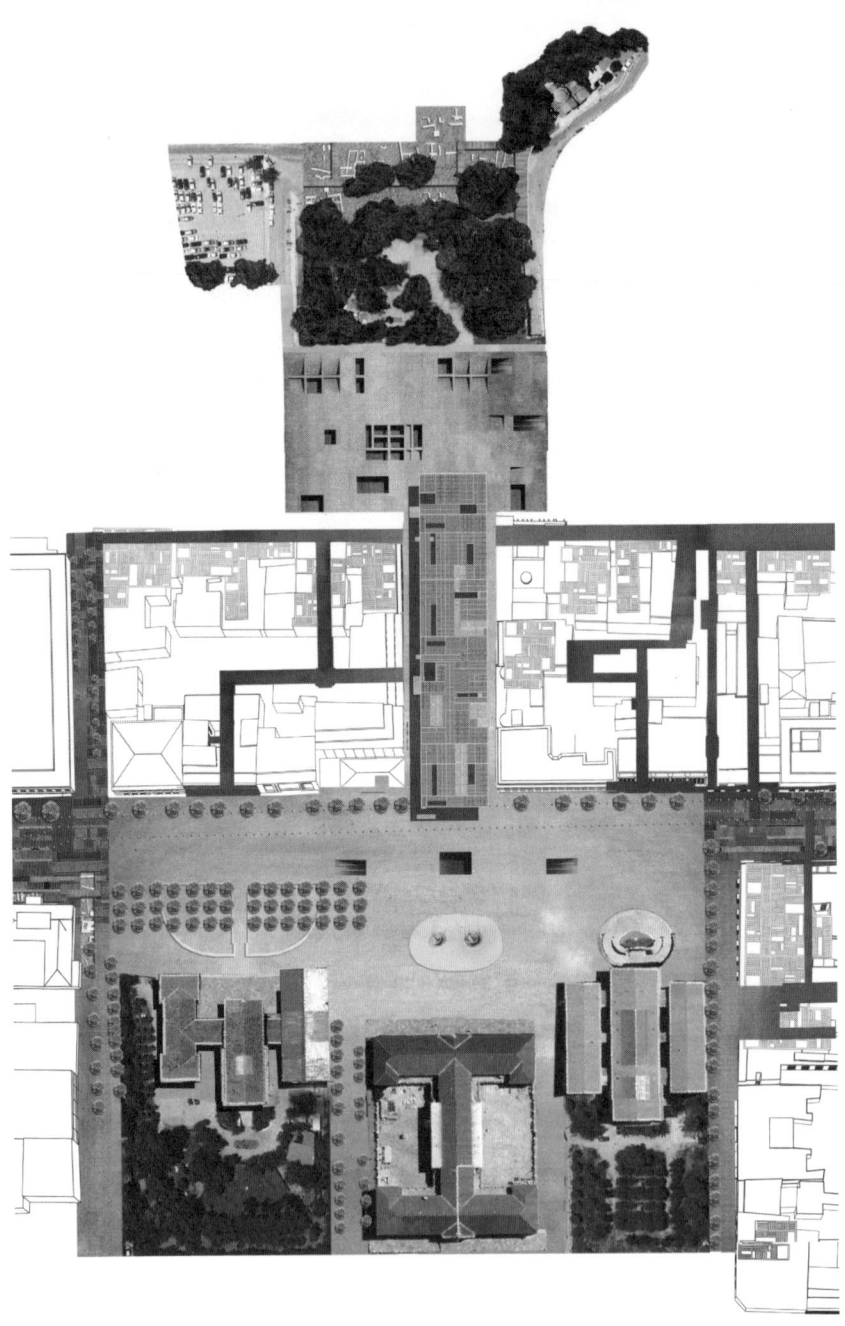

133   The Trench and the Arcade

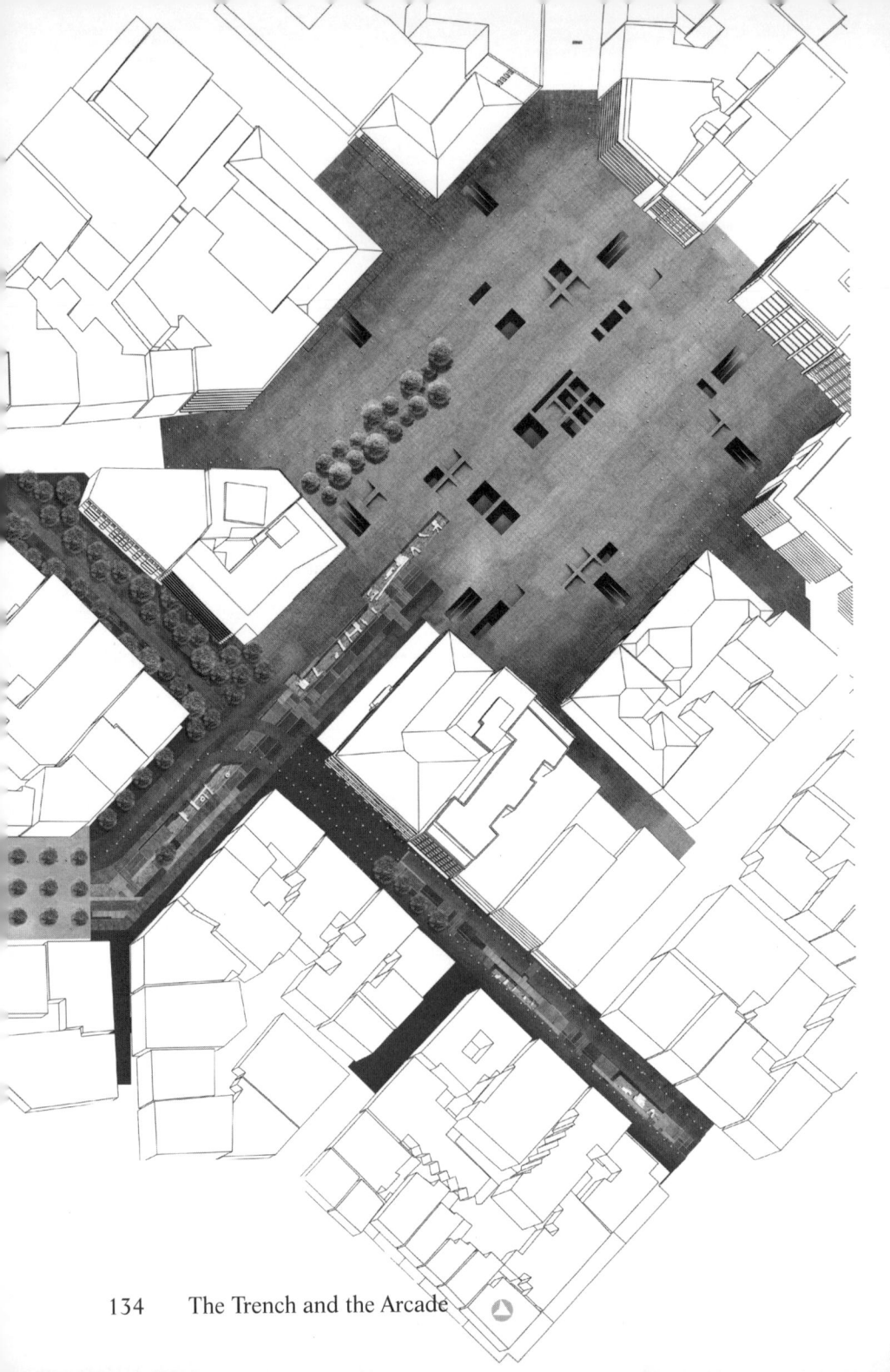

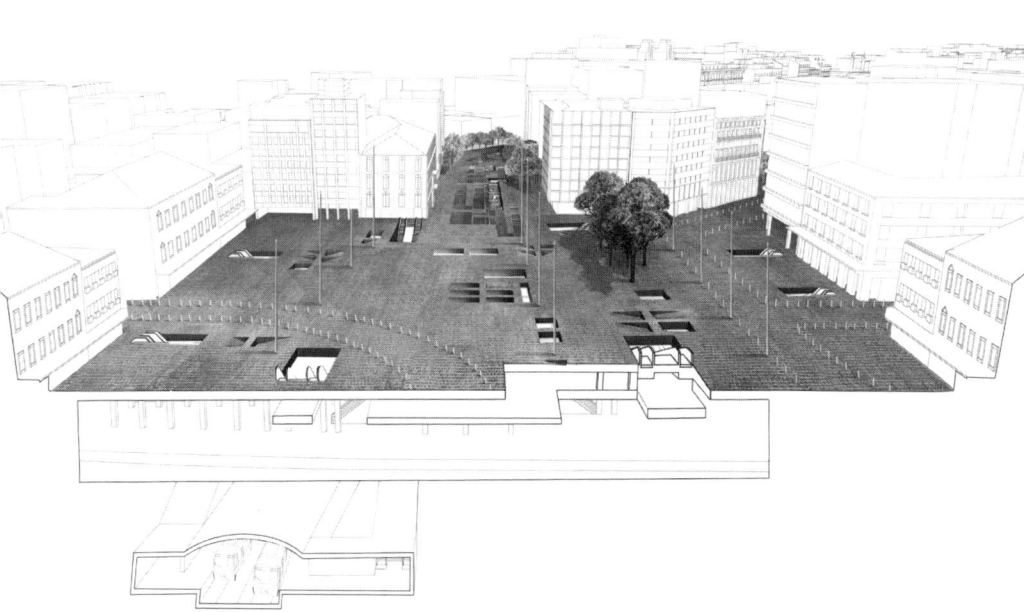

Some urban 'hole' includes archeological sites, but also existing subterranean spaces of the modern city, like metro stations and parking spaces. Thus, by introducing a different type of "archaeology", one that constitutes a spatial strategy documentation of the findings, the project leads towards some practices of urban subtraction that constitute the core of the proposal.

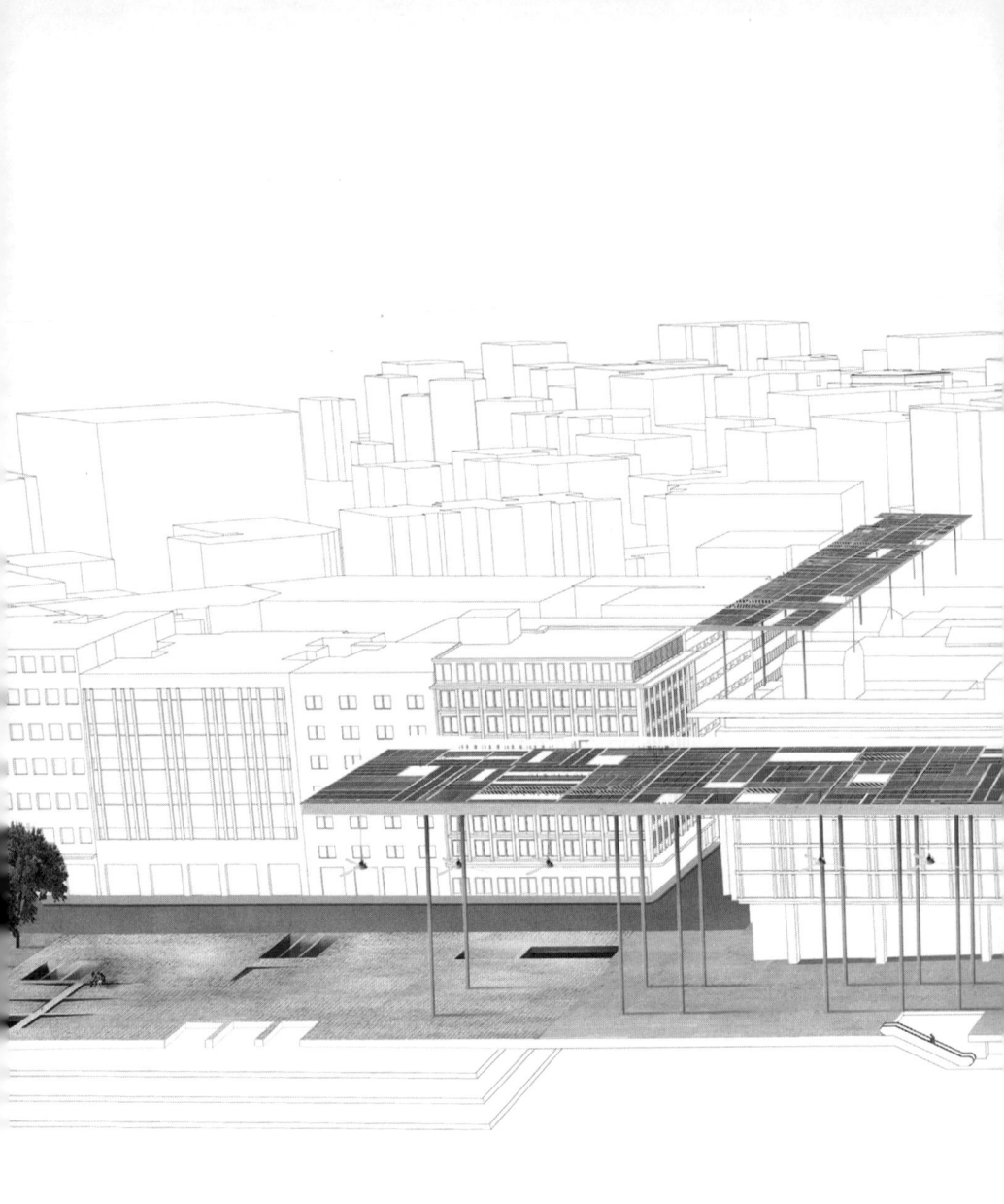

The Trench and the Arcade

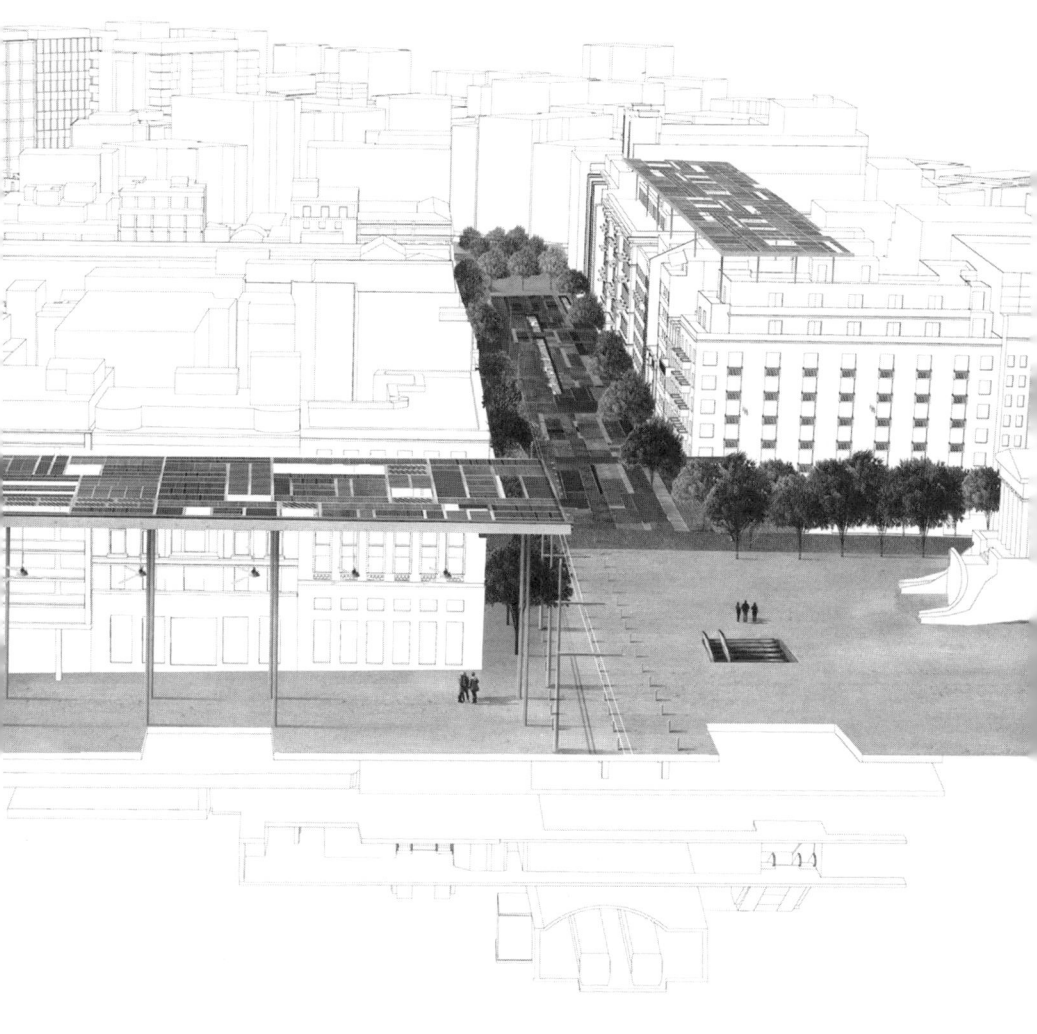

137   The Trench and the Arcade

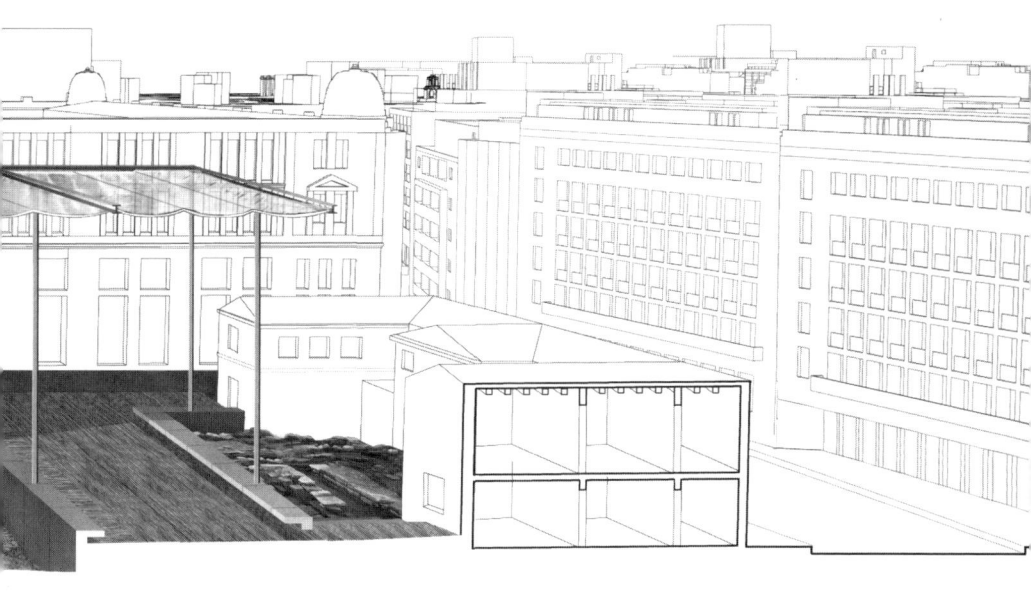

139   The Trench and the Arcade

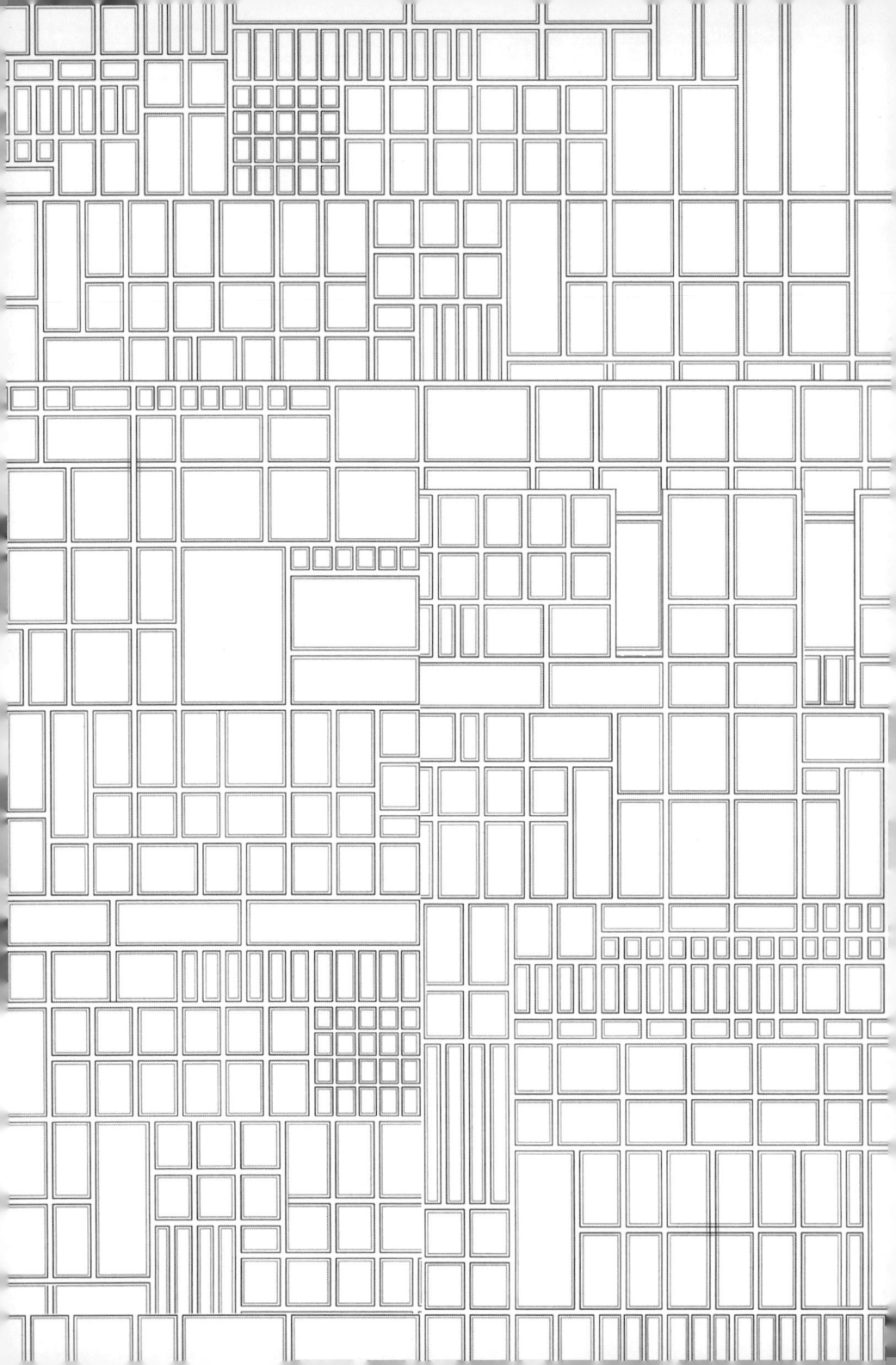

141   The Trench and the Arcade

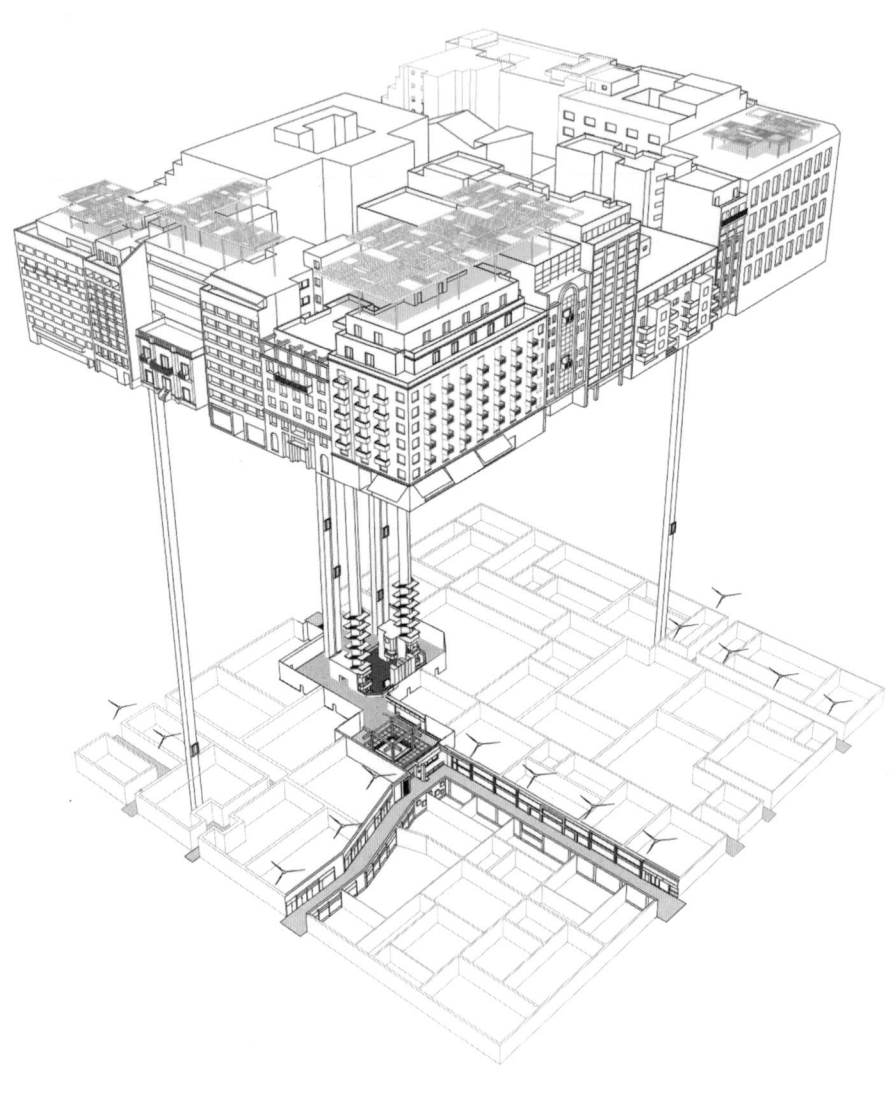

The Trench and the Arcade

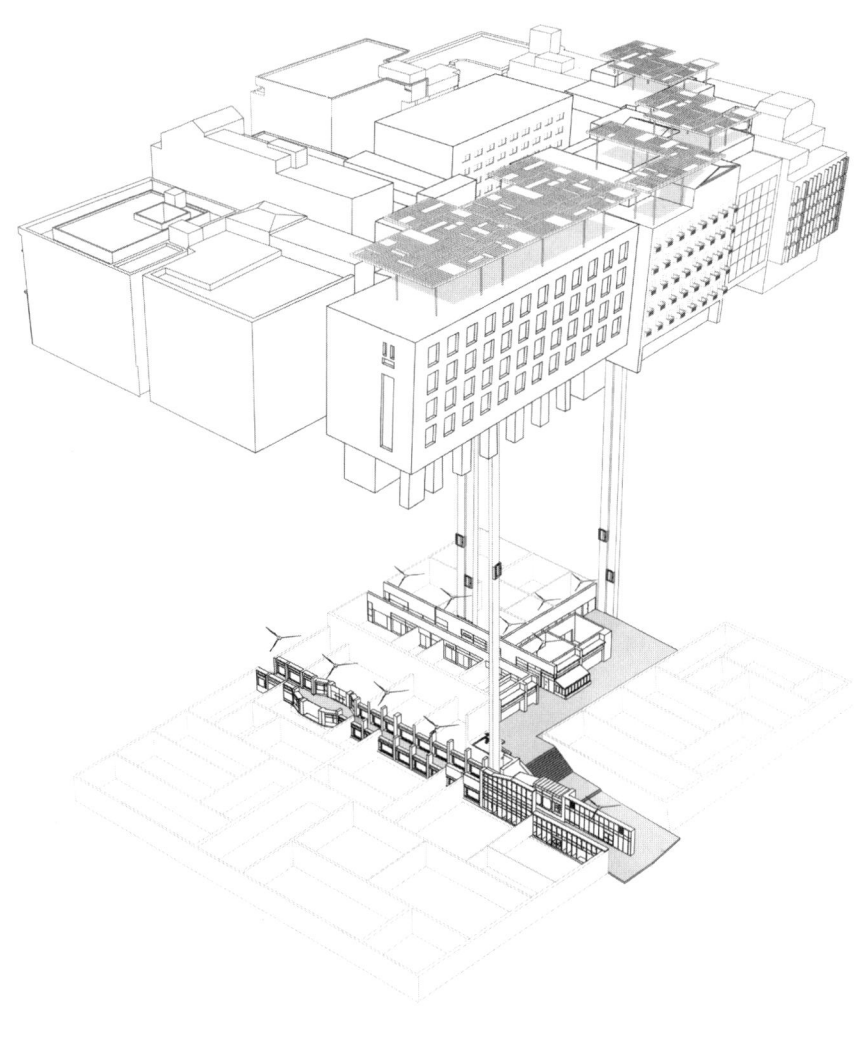

143   The Trench and the Arcade

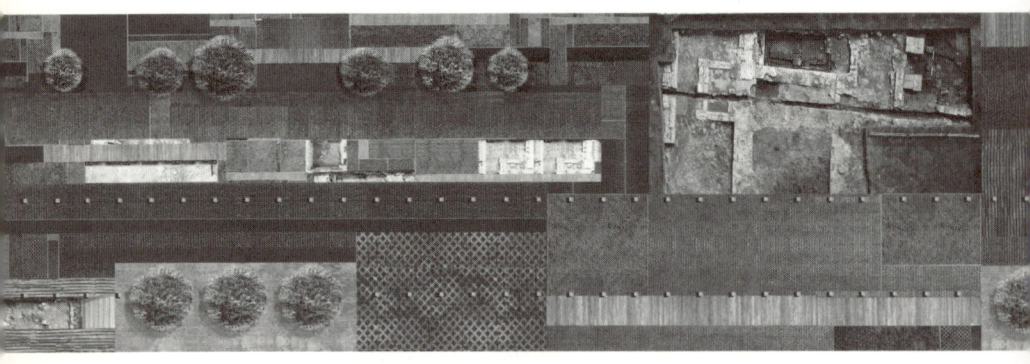

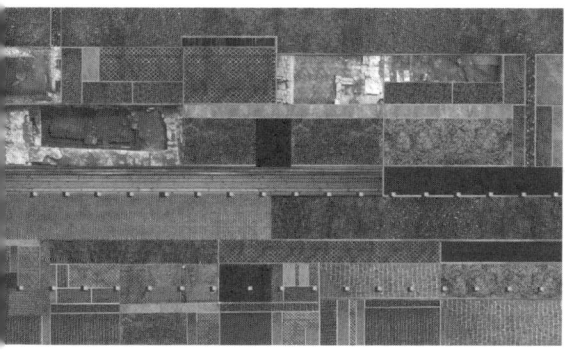

145   The Trench and the Arcade

The Trench and the Arcade

149   The Trench and the Arcade

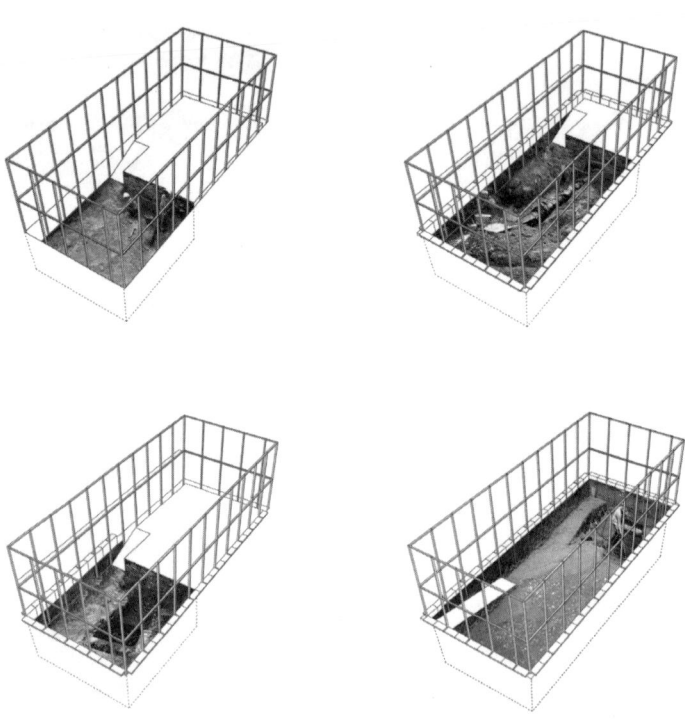

Urban Hall

The right to program and use the public space defined as the regulatory functions of the Urban Hall and the legal occupation of a public space set up as a urban apparatus that receives multiple programs through decisions of a common Internet site; multiple performances of common use can be hosted at the Urban Hall. The Urban Hall is understood as a device interacting via the Internet with the local conditions. The project is based on the protocol of the definition of a common, programmable plateau in a legally occupied space.

155   Urban Hall

A public space is challenged as a theatrical experience; protocols are scripts of future theater plays and can be performed in the Urban Hall.

159   Urban Hall

The Urban Hall platform suggests that there is always a necessity to fill with new functions empty parts of the city. In a way it shows a possibility to operate with a political agenda through filling empty urban spaces.

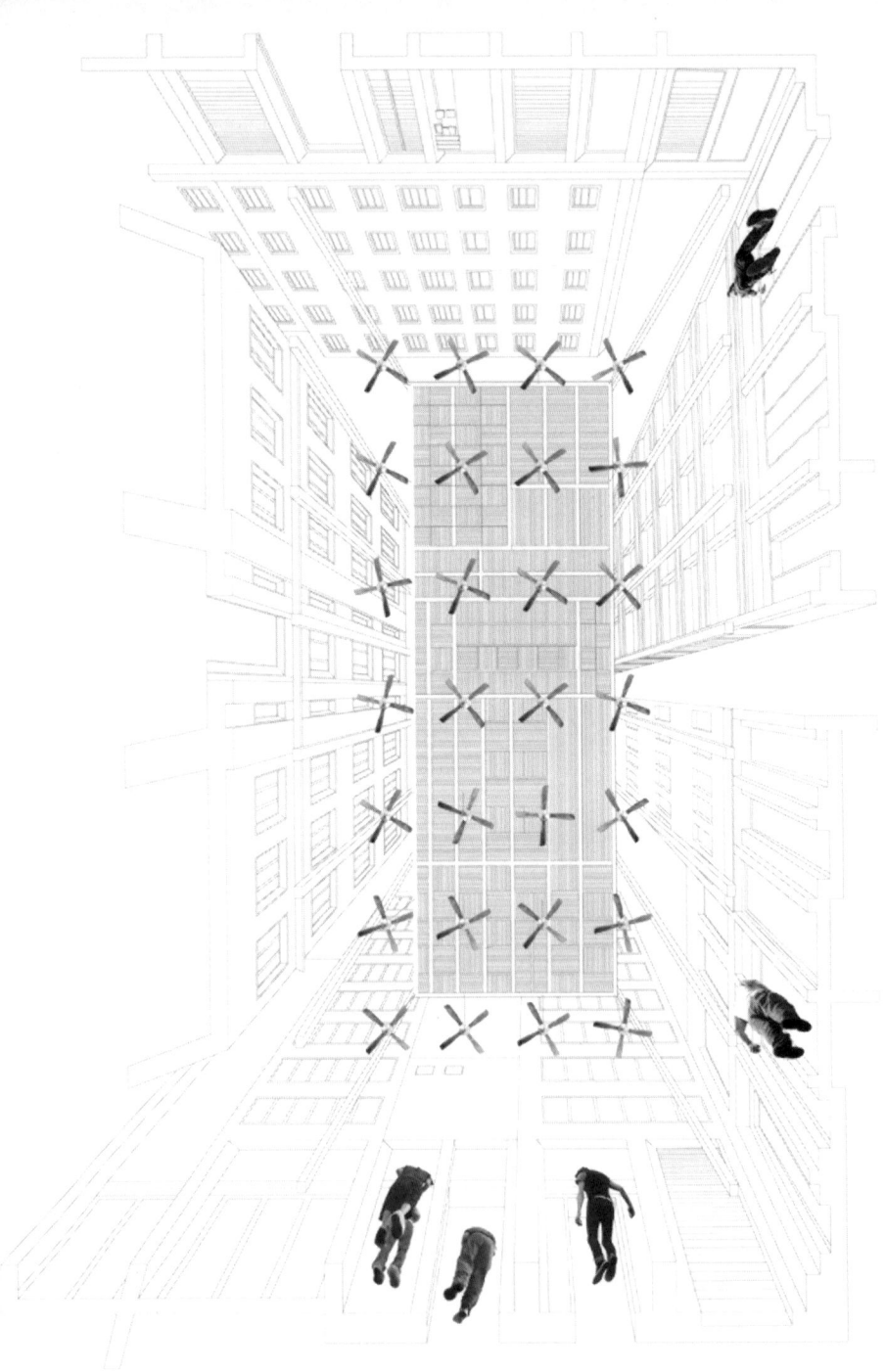

163   Urban Hall

4.11.05 ΑΓΑΠΗ ΚΑΙ ΕΝΟΧΗ:

Ένίοχρι, ένοχος είναι εκείνος που οφείλει, ο οφειλέτης εκείνος που χρωστ... Η Καλοσύνη είναι κάποιο είδος ενοχ... Ο καλός άνθρωπος είναι ο ενοχικός, ... νομίζει ότι οφείλει, επότε κι όταν ... δεν στοιχειοθετείται ... καμιά ενοχή ... χωρίς να έχει δανεισθεί επειδή είναι βαθιά ριζωμένο στην αιώνια αρχ... στον άλλο ως απαραίτητο πρόσωπο χωρίς το οποίο αδυνατεί να αγαπ... Δεν θέλει να κοιτάξει τον άλλο στην ελικρινειά του, του προσφέρει όσο περισσότερα (όπως ο έρωτας τον χαμένον χρόνον στον "άλλοτε") ελπίζοντας πώς μόνον έτσι, μόνον με τη θυσία της αυτοπροσφοράς, ο άλλος ενδεχ... να μπορεί να σταματήσει.

Αναρωτιέμαι αν αυτή η οικονομία προσφοράς που βασίζεται στην ... είναι αγάπη.

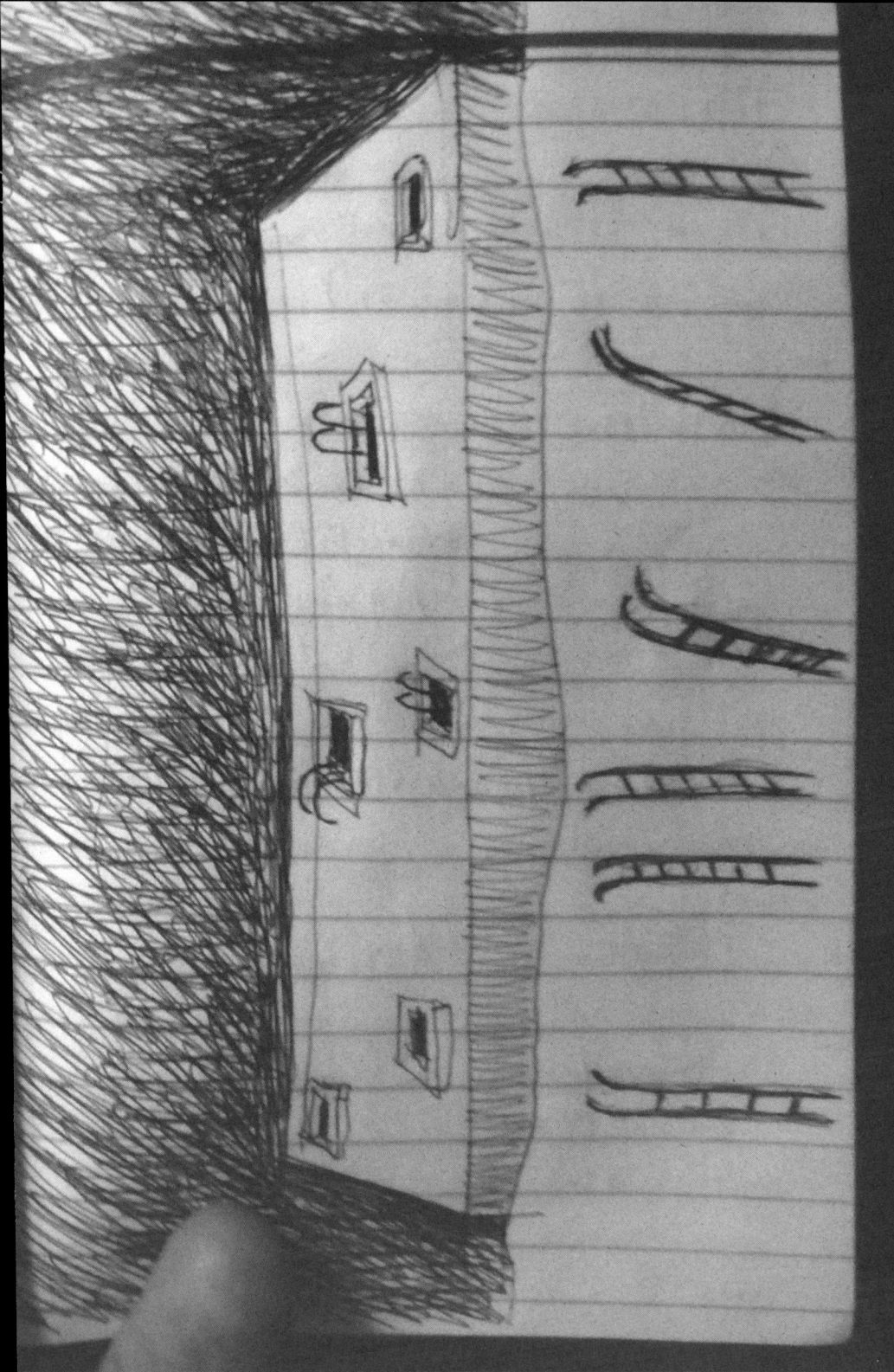

- Athens Terraces

- Terrace Playground
  ~ protocor ~

- Urban Hall

- Athens trenches
  weak monumental

- Athenian dig
  underground

- Athens/toilets

- Piraeus Tower

- Meteorite Unit

- Urban debris bench
  - open air office
  - Agglomeration of empty shops

vor

unter

aus (d)

durch

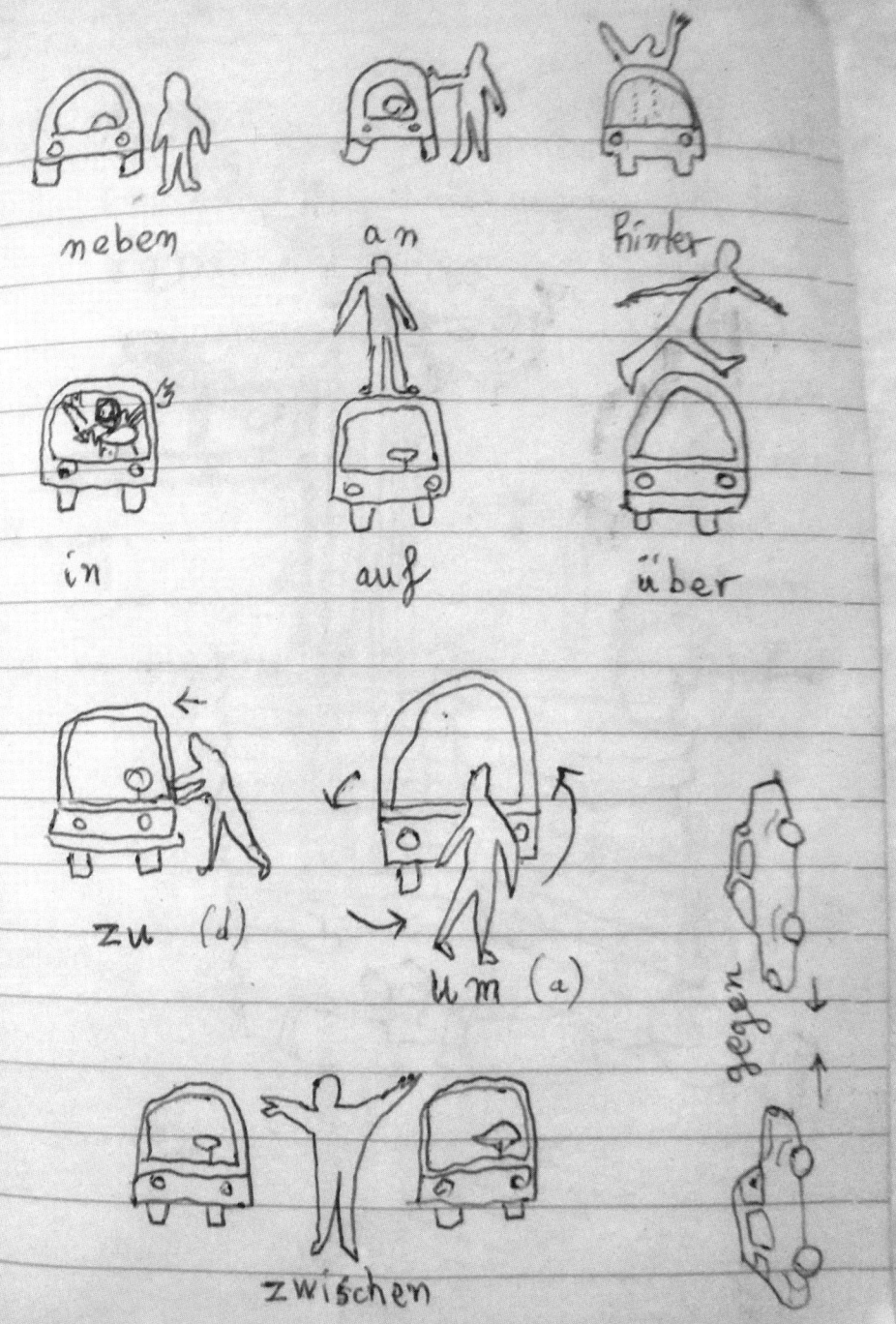

neben   an   hinter

in   auf   über

zu (d)   um (a)   gegen

zwischen

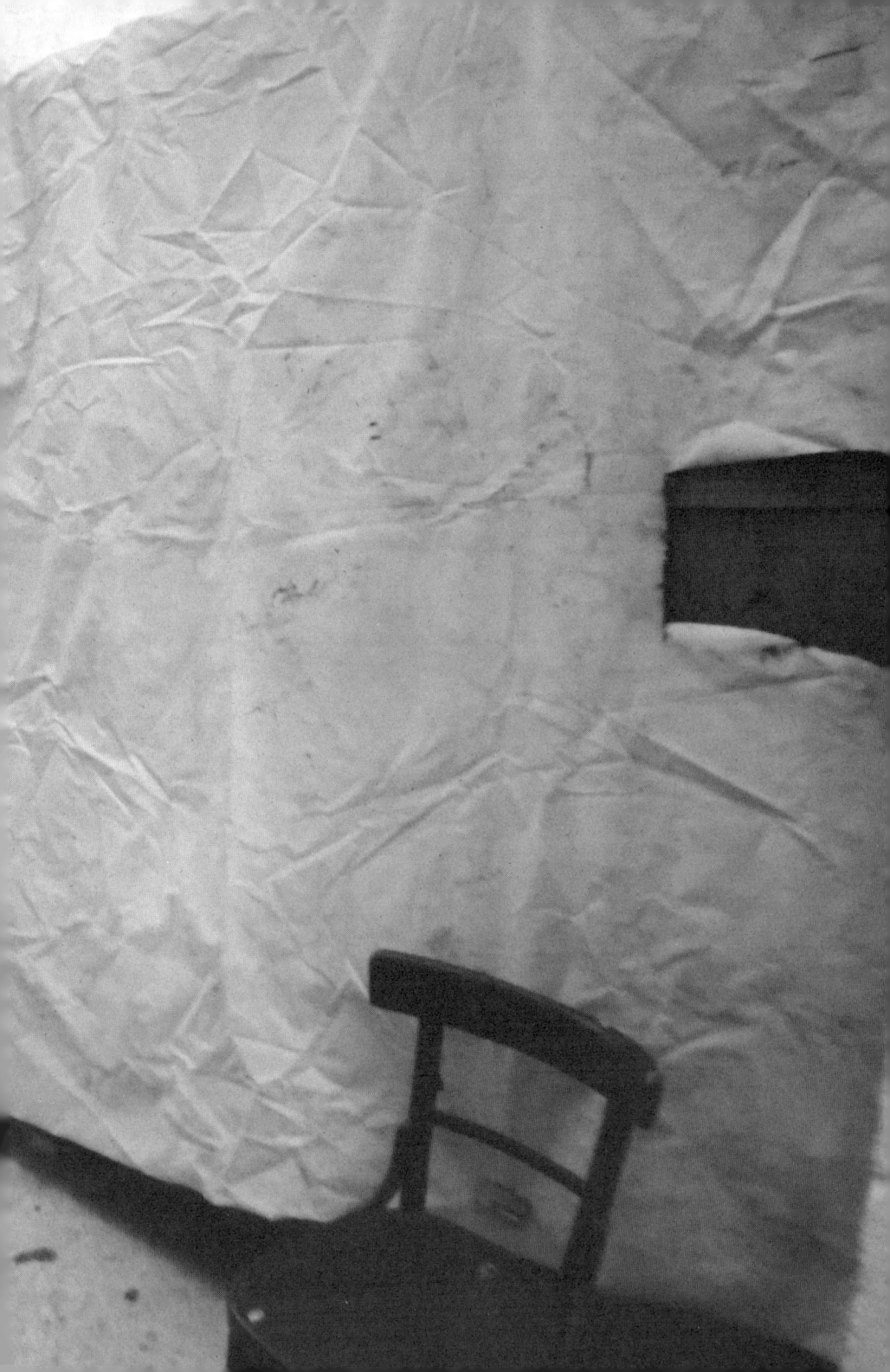

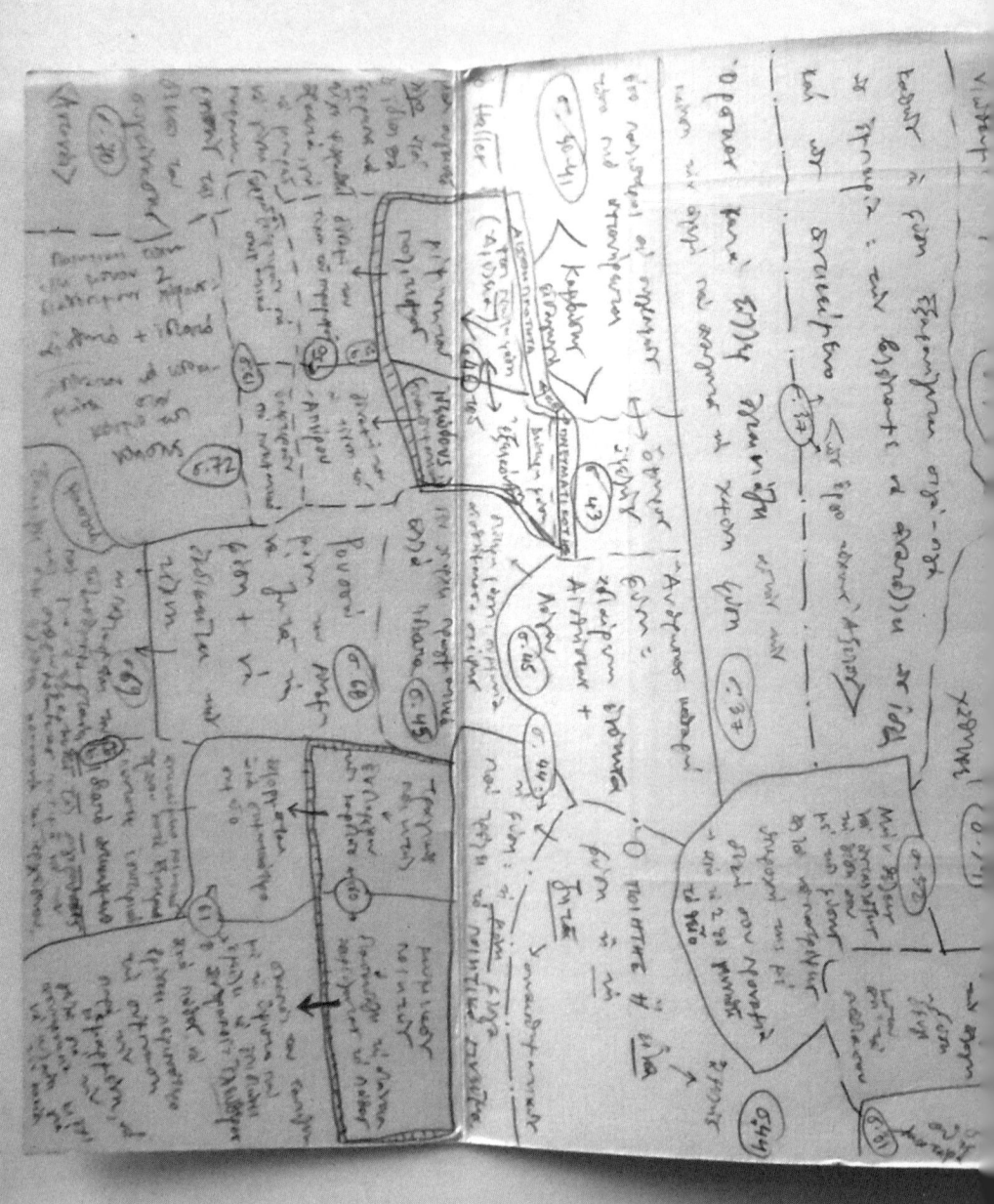

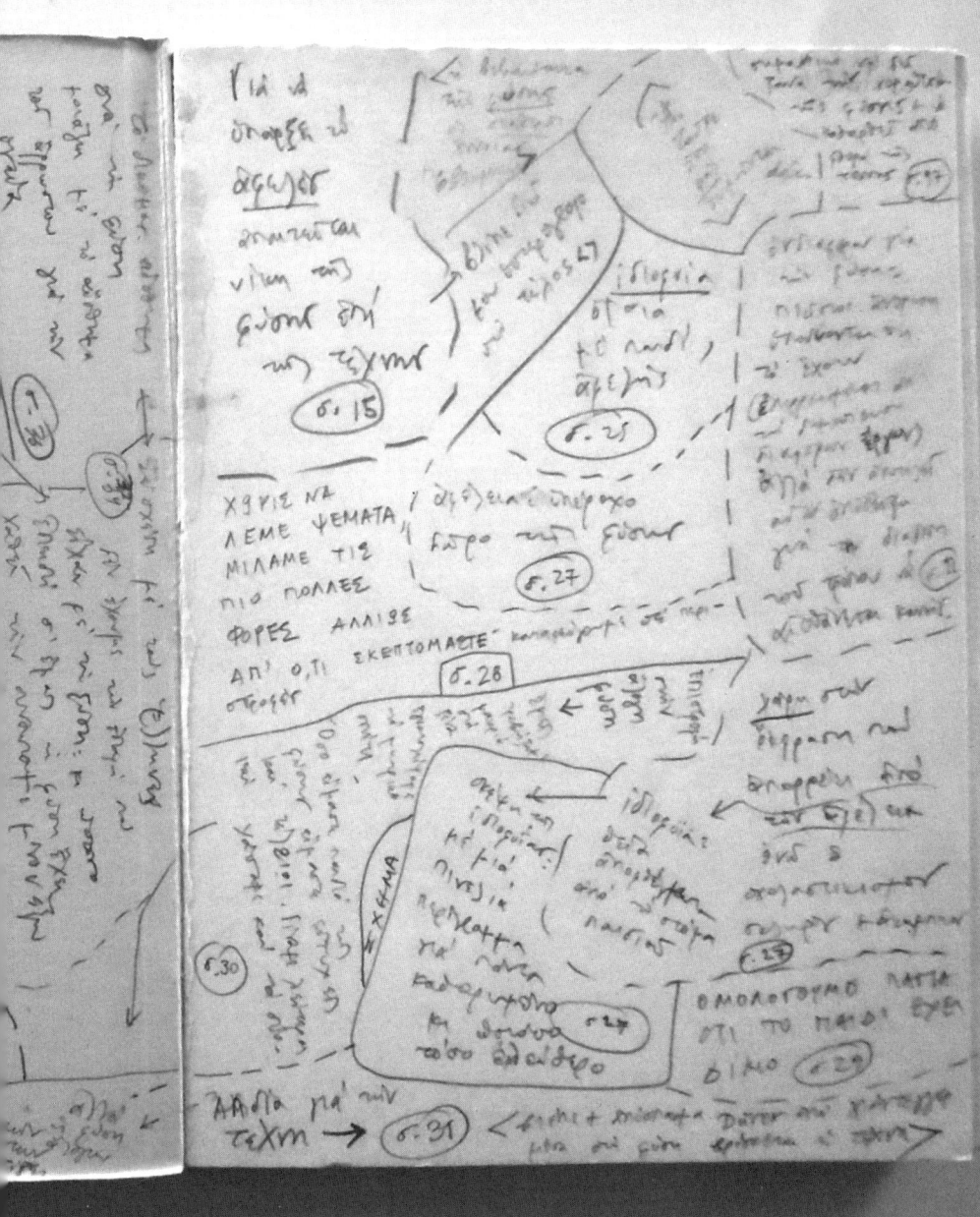

Athena Athanasiou

Designs,

desires,

distractions,

dispositions

"Poetry no longer imposes itself; it exposes itself." [1]

Aristide Antonas' edge-pushing and uniquely inventive *oeuvre* calls established questions into question. Postfoundational and disorienting, it persistently redirects our attention. In doing so, it recasts redirected, and divided the attention as a mode of attractiveness towards something other than the required, predictable or recognizable object of focus. It is, like all diversions and distractions often are, a moment of great intensity and novelty. This is about an interrupted and undecidable attentiveness, a spacing, which breaks with the contemplation/distraction opposition and lies persistently in the open; one that inscribes, if it in-scribes anything, an openness-to-come: an exposure that is constantly overflowing and deterritorializing, pushing toward the future. In Antonas' universe, this exposure emerges as both an affective disposition and a critical methodology. It emerges, in a word, as a counterpath.

Antonas calls our attention to the formation of new concepts and new uses in order to suspend both concepts and uses, in order to render them inappropriable to the closures of totalizing representation and exegesis. His Urban Protocols signify an open assemblage of digitality, affectivity, network aesthetics, and embodied spatiality. They invite us to a thought experiment, or a strategy, that is at once space-creating (i.e., occupancies of public space) and space-defying (i.e., digital prostheses and performances transcending the constraints of physical space). Furthermore, they invoke a mix of pragmatism and utopianism; a confluence of means and meanings as well as real and virtual; and a transreal engagement with the not-yet-here. Part manifesto, part archive of futurity, part ironic device, and part an open laboratory for political imagination, they stand as a provisional tool that allows one to experience and experiment with the uncanny arts of failure and reinvention. They might be best described by the term *dispositif*, in Foucault's sense, denoting simultaneously and inextricably an apparatus and a disposition. Taken together, these two etymological strands imply the process and the tendency of bringing into effect: an openness to the possibility of bringing into effect. In a word, *poesis*. This is, I think, where and how Antonas' Urban Protocols take place; in the space and in the form of a poetry that exposes itself.

This actual critical intervention –conceived both as *techne* and disposition— is nothing short of necessary today in order to engage in a collective re-thinking of crisis in its multilayered implications for urban livability. Thus we might ask: what sorts of (re)in(ter)vention would the Urban Protocols assume and entail? How would they appropriate and dis-place the conditions of urban livability within and against the exigencies of global capital? What would their collective poetics bring forth and through, what kinds of intersections of body and technology, digitality and spatiality, desires and designs? What possibilities and opportunities are there to rethink our shared (or, non-shared) categories of politics, resistance, life, and community?

And, finally, is there space left for such *unhomey* and subversive intimacies today, in a world of crisis, and, more specifically, in the current Greek neoliberal state of exception? Antonas' work seeks to do precisely that: leave (or create) space for the eventness of singular plural relationality in the polis, and in the face of losing a place, a home, a community, the right to assemble, hope, or one's means of livelihood; and thus reaffirm, in countless and incalculable ways, the unconditionality of a public hospital, a music scene, a public broadcaster, a park, a school, a theatre space.

The current Greek regime of crisis management, or, more accurately, the current regime of governing through crisis management*, brings forth the (economized, indebted, gendered, sexed, and racialized) body as a political arena of performativity and precarity. Crisis becomes an assemblage of power where politics turns into (individualistic, national and familial) securitization of bodies and societies according to the norms that underlie the condition of "becoming precarious". At the same time, the "unmarked universal" of economic management, which is a central technology of neoliberal governmentality, becomes a way to conceal the modes of differential exposure to injury, and to exclude all critical epistemologies of crisis. The state of unending crisis is a way to regulate what lines of thought and what forms of the political are made permissible and possible.

Thus, one way to engage with it might be to push crisis to its own critical limits: to deconstruct its own economy –understood as both accounting and logic. Would that be about provoking a crisis of crisis? Would it amount to an attempt to think something other than the crisis —a crisis which is not critical enough? In his engagement with Husserl's reflection on the malaise of European culture as crisis[2], Jacques Derrida suggested that "perhaps we are enduring a tremor... something other, in any case, than a crisis of reason, *beyond* a crisis of science or of consciousness, *beyond* a crisis of Europe, *beyond* philosophical crisis..."[3]

Perhaps we are enduring a tremor, a tremor that impels us to think of crisis beyond its own logics and logistics. Through their provisional methodology of intensified critical utopianism, the *Urban Protocols* suggest in many ways the question of critical epistemologies of crisis. And they situate this question(ing) squarely in present-day Athens as a site (or counter-site) for enacting a future potentiality. This is a strategy that ultimately becomes a performative call to step out of the normative time and space of crisis and to think, envision, and enact our times differently. In this sense, an ecstatic temporality is operative here, which is enacted in terms of the conditions of possibility for the making-present of the not-yet. Ecstasy, or ekstasis (*ex-stare* in Latin), as we know, represents a move outside of the (individualistic, enclosed, complacent, autarchic) self: to stand outside of oneself and its habitual, intelligible, existing order. It thus entails a mode —but also a node— of collective contemplation and becoming.

What then are the implications today of standing and taking a stance outside of oneself and in public in the current context of the political and economic logi(sti)cs of late capitalism? What kinds of spaces and spacings does this standing/taking a stance envision, enable, and enact under the truth regime of crisis? What means of embodied knowledge and site-specific infrastructure would this socio-technical space-making reclaim and require?

Performing the *Urban Protocols* involves constructing public platforms for participatory desires and designs to alter the (spatial and otherwise) conditions of urban life and livability in the midst of violent dispossession, disposability, despair, abandonment, and injustice. At this moment of dissolution, a moment marked by not only crisis but also by its becoming-ordinary, the limits of the human are situated at the core of the political –including our thinking about the political. In fact, the very term 'crisis' is linked to the vicissitudes of signifying the human; its etymology suggests a definitive decision, a decisive judgment. In these times of enduring crisis as an authoritarian device of governmental immunization, emerging critical gestures and projects of relationality, plurality, and collective exposure raise, again and again, the question of the polis as a multivalent question (and decision) of be-longing and un-belonging: who belongs and who does not belong? On what condition and at what cost? Which desires and relations are considered legible and viable? Which bodies are rendered visible and whose voices can be possibly heard and publicly registered as audible?

These questions assume their singular urgency in contexts of facing a lifetime of debt, unemployment, home foreclosure, eviction, poverty, and dissolution of public health and education. At the same time, they concern the possibility of envisioning and enacting political alliances beyond the boundaries of identity politics: ongoing pursuits and enactments of non-corporate, non-commodified sites of shared vulnerability, plurality, alternative sensibility, and responsiveness;

occasions for bringing the truth of crisis into crisis; sites and performances of consolation and confrontation. To put it differently, we can trace in the *Urban Protocols* a state and condition of potentiality, which would lie beyond its hierarchical opposition to actuality, but also, at the same time, would remain irreducible to actuality and actualization.

In the context of financial austerity, state violence and authoritarianism, but also neo-Nazi and far-right violence, Antonas' *Urban Protocols* partake of, and inquire into, crisis as a matrix of intelligibility which regulates semantic, narrational, imaginary, and affective enactments, and thus, ultimately, as an occasion and a vantage point for turning contingency into a structure of incalculable possibility under conditions of impossibility.

Perhaps we are enduring a tremor, a tremor that impels us to think of crisis beyond its own logics and logistics.

1   Paul Celan. The original quote is from the German edition of Celan collected works: *Gesammelte Werke in sieben Bänden*, Frankfurt: Suhrkamp, 2000.

2   Edmund Husserl, The Crisis of European Sciences and Transcendental Phenomenology. Trans. David Carr. (Evanston, IL: Northwestern University Press, 1970).

3   Jacques Derrida, Rogues: Two Essays on Reason, Trans. Pascale-Anne Brault and Michael Naas. (Stanford, CA: Stanford University Press, 2005), p. 124.

*   Editor's note
This essay was written before Syriza won the Greek elections in January 25th, 2015. But even now, the IFKAT – the institutions formerly known as the troika – tries to govern through the crisis.

The Script and the City

A Conversation

between

Aristide Antonas

and

Andreas Rumpfhuber

AR The visual language of your projects seems very dark, sinister
     and sometimes even dystopic. Projects like the vertical mobile
village you propose in Hymettus in Athens, but also the Urban Hall,
or your Hotel Bus project seem to have been wrested out of some
1980s science fiction novel like the *Neuromancer* trilogy of William
Gibson. They somehow seem to tell from a world in which humans
are inescapably connected to electronic machines; but your projects
also seem to tell a story of a world whose economy has gone hyperreal,
leaving its inhabitants with the debris of reality.

At the same time it seems, that your projects comment on a specific 1980s discourse in architecture. Whereas some of the 1980s architects are obsessed with the drawing and become fundamentalists by confusing the drawing, the representation, with reality, your project's drawings are different. You use the architectural drawing as an intellectual instrument of commentary and critique. Your drawings test the drawing as a tool to interpret and intervene in reality. Your drawings point to aspects of our contemporary situation. Yet I am interested in the question of how the architectonic drawing can change the world. Is the drawing already the intervention, the moment of communication?

AA Drawings are for me starting utterances, propositions similar to
        phrases. I do not like to think that in the office we do *beautiful*
drawings. Many of our friends love us for our drawings and it is true I cannot escape a certain aestheticism. Nevertheless if you want a quick answer I would of course say "No": a drawing by itself cannot change the world. We have to consider a drawing as a system of different factors. An architectural drawing is always presented in a double bind: it explains something as a concrete promise but it also never gets concrete enough. It formalizes the answer to a technical problem but it remains definitively unable to stand in the place of the represented. Representation always fails to substitute the represented; this is its definitive rule; it is proposed as a mourning of something envisioned and necessarily lost.

Our last work constructs urban propositions related to constructed representations of the Athenian landscape. We construct representations of the city and we confront them. At the scale we normally work it seems to be difficult to architecturally articulate a political strategy. Yet the proposals have always the ambition to be expendable and exemplary. They can be repeated or reprogrammed in the form of benevolent viruses. This is what I consider to be the most challenging part of the work; its possible iterations. Athens center provides us with an emblematic area of dereliction and abandonment whose infrastructure could still function. I think about Athens city center as a ghost-like infrastructure field; the infrastructure stands vertically, unable to be used since the city center is emptied. We negotiate with the possibilities of sharing it again – yet now in different ways. In this sense drawing is a compromise and a practical system of reference. It is a language. We usually consider architecture as a simple function of walls and openings, a series of stably posed obstacles; walls, columns and floors. Obstacles are cut in sections and plans. They are drawn in traditional drawings. This is what Architecture will always be related to; it remains linked to the most stable parts of buildings and their construction. But we are today interested to investigate different stabilities that could generate *different concepts of function* in architecture. To what extend can we program a situation? Most of my projects' drawings present a simple protocol and its specific application; my protocol is a theater script and the drawings intend to present the script's staging. I consider the work we do in the office as the promise for a strangely scripted city. In the drawings we depict "still-frames" of the protocol's performance. The protocol, its specific background and some material additions stage this complex and sometimes invisible architecture. The moment captured in the drawings has to be thought as a random but indicative result of a performed script.

Urban processes are seen as open-ended theater play scripts, shapeable by simple rules and by the use of certain objects; the contemporary city functions already as an accumulation of distinct, separate, cluster-like mini structures. In my role as a script-writer I collaborate with law specialists in order to shape the proposed, idiosyncratic, theatrical experience; we discuss together with them about the prescription of a protocol and its expected distortions in the city's status quo. How can we intervene in the specific field of the Greek law? What rules could perform what condition? What type of micro legislation do we need in order to program parts of the urban space? How a piazza can be converted to something different through the intermediation of a minimal legislative layer. How can we shape architecture as a legislative regulation? Usually my drawings present some possible moments of the performance of a rule; the impossibility to show the "rule itself" drives to this strategy for the drawings. Sometimes we cannot show more than some paradigmatic moments that capture the performance of the the protocol; if we only wrote down the protocol as a text we would be more precise and more technical than using the drawing. Yet we would miss something. We need the 3D drawings, the sections and the plans in order to translate the protocols into a different language. Some technical data concerning the buildable parts of the interventions and some perspective views correspond to the proposals we do. We use the tradition of architecture in order to investigate about the city. Adopting the language of the architect's discipline is part of this strategy. Another part of the work is related to some necessary changes in the discipline itself. Yoshiharu Tsakamoto from Atelier Bow Wow once suggested that the architect is a witness of what is happening. For him, architects do not change radically a situation, they intervene by being there and they undertake this strange, intermediary role of the witness. They are an important part of the situation; not the victim nor the perpetrator but a witness of what is happening, maybe witness of a crime under execution. The witness is always posed in a certain distance from what he observes but also in a constitutive nearness to what is happening. Being a witness is not an easy role. We can shape differently this concept of architectonic witnessing while acting as architects today; witnessing refer to the construction of a condition. We are responsible about how we observe. We are not passive while observing. The question is "how cunning a responsible witness can be?" This is the question of today's architecture because architects affect the situation they are witnessing. Architects are obliged to respect limits and yet they are not exactly out of the situation. Witnessing supports a series of relations to a situation; the witness may intervene into the situation's setting, it may act as an aggressive force by refusing action or it may slightly distort the situation in which the observation takes place. Witnessing brings us already to an art of observing; this art can create different situations out of the given. The architect enters the situation with a certain responsibility. Architects are not only charged to follow the rules of their commissions. They are supposed to shape what they observe to something interesting at a different level, staying cynical *vis-à-vis* any expectation. Architecture is valuable if it offers different readings of a situation not if it only executes correctly a commission. Serving the society in reproducing itself is not the curse of the architect.

You see why, having said all that, the question about drawing becomes one of the most important issues for me. Drawings are intellectual matter. But they are not supposed to be framed and admired on a wall; they constitute a part of my notes, destined to organize an intention, like the pages of books. I am interested in the distortions of the real; the drawings we do in my office cannot show the transformations that we envision for a city; but in order to expand the architectonic language, in order to enrich its programmatic part we chose this way of operating. In Russian constructivism the invented programs had immediate relation to new type of constructions. Nowadays in Athens we have to invent programs for already existing spaces. A different type of Aldo Rossi's "scena fissa" is the base of our investigation; we are obliged to live in these modern remains.

The drawings work in a similar way to the message that a terrorist group leaves after an attack: technical architecture data capture some subcutaneous "attack" to the given normalities of the city. After a terrorist attack we receive sometimes this message explaining why a bomb exploded in a location. Well, sometimes I also try to explain what we do with short texts that accompany the drawings; it is the analogue to this normal terrorist practice. I think that art and terrorism share a lot in common mostly in the way they handle the possibility of meaning; they force us to receive messages. Neither art nor such attacks described as terroristic pretend us to think so much, but only to accept a point of view. Art is not always like this; but we find more and more art-projects pressing us to adopt ready-made moral propositions as facts. That's when art becomes didactic in a sense I cannot accept. Preconceived or ready-made meaning will always be my most frightful enemy. It drives directly to murders and idealizations. We only can accept or reject; this is the decay of "discourse" per se. I refer to the word "terrorism" only because it is controversial; it is used in order to scare; naming an act terroristic has also a terroristic part. The way a message is received and circulated today is not isolated by what we normally understand as a terrorist way of acting. What I try to do with our work is to use the power of a strong representation only to lead to the contrary result – an open space for thought: a consciously heavy representation can destabilize a given situation. This is how I try to contribute to a societal discourse through architecture. Maybe it is an impossible task. I use the power of a first estrangement only in order to give space to a reflexion. My victim would always be normality and in this first moment I ought much to the tradition of modernism; but *Unheimlichkeit* is not a target per se for me; I propose different scripts for normality. In this busy and thoughtless environment I cannot remain silent; I do not use any of the given organized systems of already canalized resistance; I try to think about possible action in given conditions. It is always about the appropriate way to engage in a radically experimental way, to think about different, possible forms of acting than simply refusing the existing; to lead to more languages for architecture; to write with drawings or to direct the normal practice of architecture towards a different side. I try to stay practical and confront what is going on while the condition of Athens changes; it is a privileged place to think about the decline of western civilization. Athens is the place of western decay par excellence. If the web is not understood as an already constituting legislative power we will not realize and not be able to shape urban transformations that could follow. Urban protocols are here to concretize the relation between the net and the remains of urban space.

AR   When you refer to your projects as readings of a contemporary urban situation, that your projects actually are investigations into the specific contemporary condition of Athens, I immediately have to think of the Open-Air Office. In this project you offer tables and seating, office lights at night and free WiFi and water in an empty urban situation. I read this project as a spatial commentary in order to investigate one aspect of our contemporary societal situation and its labour conditions. Many have argued that this situation needs to be traced back to the late 1960s and early 1970s; that it is related to the dissolvement of the Bretton Woods Treaty, unleashing the economic logic from gold (from real matter). In many respects this created an immaterial economy directly affecting our way of living together. There are fantastic and insightful analysis of the very situation in critical theory describing this new and emerging capitalism: Late-Capitalism or Neo-capitalism as Theodor W. Adorno in 1969 and Frederic Jameson in 1997 would call it, Cognitive Capitalism as named by Moulier Boutang (2007), or Finance Capitalism as Christian Marazzi (2007) termed it.

Luis Suarez-Villa called it the Techno-Capitalism and just recently Paul B. Preciado intriguingly called it Pharmacopornographic Capitalism in his fantastic book *Testo-Junkie* (2013). The Open-Air Office seems to play with the spatial organization of an urban situation that is defined by our contemporary economic situation.

AA You are right, the inconvertibility between gold and dollar
   that Nixon declared in 1971 is invisibly related to this Athenian investigation. Maurizio Lazzarato considers the moment of this dissociation from gold as the historical moment that transformed money into debt. Money stops to be anchored to a material reference. In parallel the reality's relation to facts and things becomes blurred after this abstraction. And to me this situation reverberates powerfully to architecture. The value of materiality is transformed. Abstraction takes command in the form of a systematic, ruled direction of situations. Space becomes more and more the beholder of stable, invisible, immaterial structures. We do not see what happens; at the contrary what we see is what doesn't happens; we see somebody in front of a screen but we do not know where the screen viewer is, the screen viewer becomes the ghost of an invisible reality. There is another level of investigation we need to engage ourselves in order to understand what is going on when we see people siting in front of networked screens. The Open-Air Office intervenes in such a situation by stating its ambivalent status. It shows a plural group of people siting together but not taking under consideration their co-presence in many ways. We intended to condense this idiosyncratic condition of "individual presence being unimportant" in a large scale. Yet I don't know if "condensing" is the correct word concerning this phenomenon. The word condensation may lead to the Heideggerian concepts and I want to stay at a distance from it today. Maybe some dilution would better to name the Athens case. This dilution I am envisaging has to do with an ongoing indifference about hierarchy and articulation in the structural level that could concern ensembles. Condensation refers to a concrete whole and to an operating center of a thing or a phenomenon, dilution is already introduced as a rationalization of decay. Accumulations are more important than compositions; the parts that structure a diluted

condition are in this case isolated and temporarily self sufficient.
We cannot easily operate in a traditional architectonic way in such a
situation. At the Open Air Office it is transposed and reshaped a well
known condition in a vacant area of the empty city center. We never see
this condition as such but we know it; we imagine easily a picture of the
inhabitants of a city, sitting at tables and working; it is only the city we
know without walls: this image is a representation of the most banal and
boring urban normality. But when it is transposed to a public space and
when it is shown as part of the common ground it is transformed to an
uncanny image. We are familiar to the Open Air Office and yet we do
not know why. We do not know what is really common in it; why does
this setting of operating infrastructure projected on a background of
modern ruins is so familiar to us. The common theme in today's city can
concern us if it is displaced. The Open Air Office is an elaboration of
the traditional Athenian open air cinema; there is no obvious common
interest for many people to watch altogether a single film. At the
contrary, everyone watch their own screen; we lose the common point
of interest; we lose the disposition in parallel rows. Kubelka's invisible
cinema was maybe a part of the same story. Well, now everybody has
a screen that shows different content; we have to invent a community
while the separation is operated by a radical division of interest. The
community could now be organized at the necessary co-presence
that happens usually in offices. We work at our own project, we enjoy
our own way. An open air salon for immaterial labor! In that sense it
relates to your research, Andreas; the *Bürolandschaft*, the Fun Palace,
and other projects of the 60's that you are writing about in your book
are my precedents. Furthermore: the Open Air Office is realized as an
idiosyncratic common constitution of withdrawal. We withdraw to
our personal sphere and there is poison in this desire of the common
that performs through withdrawal. With the Open Air Office I try to
shed light to this structure of common withdrawal that substitutes
society. It is a contradictory scheme and it is stronger than the market
or the hope for a different common life. An Open Air Office functions
in both the market and the hope for change. In the Open Air Office
the users of the tables withdraw together. I try to propose this project
as a repeatable urban space for Athens and for other mediterranean

cities. As an installation it can be permanent if we change the material of the tables and some parts of the legislation concerning the Internet. Does it means that we accept or we deny the common culture of the withdrawal to the self? I am usually asked to answer this question and as you may suggest the project is the answer: I exaggerate in accepting the very fact of individual withdrawal from the common; I hope that in this way I already criticize it as a position of the nowadays imaginary. The formation of the Open Air Office confronts the exact legislative regulation under which it performs. Withdrawal, through different, changing meanings, is an important word for the constitution of a city in many ways. The Open Air Office gives a communal look to this rationale of individual withdrawal. The withdrawal of the self from the community is the only urban axiom a "nowadays society" guarantees. This may be a paradox; the Open Air Office plays with the theatrical form of this renouncement of the social; an example of a society, a script for it, staged to operate with people together while they withdraw. The juxtaposition of withdrawn people may form an impossible common space for the current city. Something may happen because of this coincidence that the Open Air Office organizes by inviting people to get together even in order to perform their individual work.

The Open Air Office is proposed as a protocol. Its first rule is structured as a technical description of its equipment; the equipment transforms it to a system of separate users gathered together in an open air space of the abandoned city center. The city's infrastructure is still there. You already described the protocol: water, WiFi, light, tables and stools. We could add some more descriptions for it; a sudden shape of a given condition; an invitation to view the hidden interior of the city; a common interior spectacle inverses in the form of an open air field; a common spectacle or a spectacle of the common. The users guess if they inhabit a new type of square or possibly an alternative office space; the city incarnates here the factory of society we already inhabit, but this condition allows us to imagine ourselves in a different protocol. We have to project to something different this distortion and this decline of the common; a different common as an expectation may still be possible. I hope that the Open Air Office already includes these descriptions of the city, these questions and this openness concerning its possible future.

195   Antonas and Rumpfhuber

I try to form the questions of the future by proposing architectural programs. I am very careful about the definitions of architecture I need in order to proceed in this direction. Part of the architect's library of buildings were done by philosophers, writers or law specialists. We could refer to Plato's cave of *the Republic*, the house of Stevenson's *Doctor Jekyll and Mr Hyde*, a room from *À la recherche du temps perdu* by Marcel Proust or the *Panopticon* of Jeremy Bentham. They present specific texts or built concepts that were produced with words; they became important due to architecture's direct relation to discourse. One needs the Panopticon, in order to proceed to Foucault's analysis of the society of control. The duration of a continuous surveillance, some different states of detention are already presented and concretized by Bentham. Without any doubt the Panopticon and its performance is already a remarkable architecture. It gives shape to a situation, and in this sense it stages an intervention to what is given. To shape a given situation, or to exaggerate it, already marks an intervention to the situation itself. A project that follows this principle of shaping a given situation can be shocking and also uncannily attractive. The radicalization, within which this condensation is presented, makes possible a violent intrusion in the condensed situation. This is my ambition for the Open Air Office and for many of my Athenian projects.

AR You referred to my *Architecture of Immaterial Labor* and it is
    true that the Open-Air Office has something to do with the examples in this book of mine. It has a direct relation to the practice of the transdisciplinary team of the Schnelles and their invention of the office landscape, but also with Cedric Price's Fun Palace, and with Hans Hollein's Mobile Office. Yet your practice in general and the Open Air Office in specific are of course also different.
    In my research about architecture of immaterial labour I focused on a historic moment – that of the 1960s. It was then that a new economic paradigm (Post-Fordism) and its new labour conditions (Immaterial Labour) become dominant in our Western industrial societies. I ask if architecture also becomes immaterial or what forms it takes on. In the examples that I use, there is still the old paradigm of a Fordist mode of production visible. But exactly through this background

it is possible to clearly decipher new emerging organizations and practices of architecture. One can start to understand what kind of forms and formations architecture has to take on, and what possibilities there are for architects, in dealing with this new societal situation.

I would ask if architecture actually only portrays the orderly appearance of works in a space of production that is rigorously defined by wage compensation? Thus: does architecture design – in the words of the French philosopher Jacques Rancière – the employment and the attributions of the spaces, onto which workers activities are distributed? Or: if the practice of architecture orders new (labour) relations, in relation to society? Are architects therefore consultants, hosts and agents of a capitalist order, or do architects affect familiar orders and distributions with the means of architecture and therefore alter its status?

I read the Open Air Office as an architectural intervention or maybe even as an architectural performance, that actually alters and reorganizes a specific situation – a situation that not only includes the physical space but also the discourses around it. And having this, it does not matter if or how people or companies would understand your alternative approach and vision of the Open Air Office. I think this is the very nature of an architectural practice that understands itself as part of society and its discourses to be immersed in it. So the project needs to stay ambivalent. In some respect the Open Air Office is like the very first Bed-In performance in Amsterdam by John Lennon and Yoko Ono. They use a given infrastructure (the Hilton hotel) and re-organize it for their own enterprise: world peace. In the very first instance of the performance in Amsterdam, they actually create a moment of re-distribution of the sensible. Amongst others they introduce a new mode of activism that is actually very passive, and journalists and the public didn't really know how to handle and how to interpret the performance. Yet in the repetition of the Bed-In in Montreal, some weeks later, this is all being corrected by the Media. This second performance is then also the one who's images we predominantly remember, and whose scripting – with all the invited guests at the bed-side of the two – is today's official story of the event: with John as the hero, Yoko the silenced woman, etc. So your Open Air Office has indeed aspects of this first staging of the Bed-In. If you would start to reproduce the Open Air Office (i.e. The Open Air Office would become a yearly event in the place) the status of the project would radically change.

AA   I would prefer it to be permanent. The Open Air Office is not proposed as an event. It is just tested for a short period. And I think that architects are neither agents of the capitalist system nor can they radically institute new orders; we work because we have the impossible mission to understand, explain and interpret. There are limits we have to respect and also opportunities to intrude into every system. We stick to the different systems rationales in order to deconstruct them seriously. A certain cynicism is part of this attitude. An interpretation does not only depend from what is given, it needs a number of decisions in order to be operated. Interpretation needs reinventions of the given as such. The decisions are related to the reading of every condition; not to a passive acceptance and elaboration of the common but rather to a conceptual reorganization of the given. Let's go back to your work about immaterial labor and architecture. It indicates a very fertile field of investigation. The buildings and the emblematic diagrams you go through in your book show programs with rare conceptual force; they shaped possible futures with an inventive, intrusive power to the systems they were reexamining in critical ways. Nevertheless they were read, built and reproduced as naive imitations of what they were proposing in their first versions; the mall type, can be understood as a problematic *Fun Palace*, and the *Bürolandschaft* supported the typical form of office working space that condensed, reproduced or exaggerated to the maximum the best exploitation of the office workers during the last decades. You propose the idea that there is a decline from the first Bed-In performance in Amsterdam to the second one, in Montreal. It is a valuable observation regarding this art installation of Yoko Ono and John Lennon. But when you say in your book together with Deleuze that "creating has always been different from communicating" and that "the key thing is to create vacuoles of non-communication, circuit breakers, so we can elude control", I have to keep a distance from you. Žižek stated in relation to an occupied park in Athens' Exarcheia area that there is no major problem for capitalism to accept such isolated circuit breakers functioning with different principles. This remark could also form a quick mediated critique to Hakim Bei's concept of Temporary Autonomous Zones. We could say they do not contradict the norm of isolated protocols around which I see the society being reorganized. They don't contradict the rationale of an Archipelago of Protocols that the capitalist order keeps shaping anyway. I have to agree with Žižek in this occasion. The idea that there is decline at the exact moment we keep a parallel relation to the market without claiming we break the relation with it, does not help. It is not practical for me. To adopt some of the market's rules can be more dangerous for the market itself than proposing ruptures that obviously can be easily incorporated or neglected by it. In my opinion, the idealization of the "circuit breakers" is then a factor that is not functional for thinking, at least concerning Athens in this particular moment; bridging with courageous legal interventions the existing situations we could reschedule the civic agenda of the city; different laws are needed, the relation of the city regulations to the Internet becomes obvious. Any social and individual emancipation can begin within the web. We accept the Internet as if it was an incontestable sphere but it is via the Internet that the new global social order is getting settled. The Internet is the example *par excellence* of an archipelago of protocols, ready to colonize the cities of tomorrow. If the Internet is not socially controlled, it will regulate individual identities and social life crudely and according to the powers that rule it; the declining legal structure of the western countries that is collapsing more or less visibly may not secure constitutional rights for the next city users. We lose much if we keep silently accepting the absence of legal basis of the transformation of the society that happens for example in Greece. Creation, circuit-breaking and independent practices cannot intrude and transform the function of a bankrupted city.

AR Well, here I need to interrupt you for a second and argue about
       what you just said and clarify my position. This concerns the role
of the architect and her or his possibility of practice in a contemporary
situation. When I refer to the "contemporary situation" I speak of a
relation between dominant economic discourses and the practice of
architecture. Since economic discourses have been expanding into

all aspects of live, I think it is not exaggerating to refer to them as
the precondition of the contemporary architectural practice per se.
It is interesting that the relationship with architecture to the various
economic discourses in history have always defined the practice of
architecture. It is peculiar that in a current academic or critical discourse
on architecture this aspect is missing, or is only touched upon by
dismissing and neglecting an economic reality. Historically seen this has
not always been the case. Durand, for example, argued with economic
means, but also in the German history of architecture people like
Friedrich Gilly and his protege Karl Friedrich Schinkel used economic
arguments not only for selling their project. Rather, economy was an
integral part of the Modern practice of architecture, a practice that, of
course, is quintessentially a bourgeois practice. Yet something radically
has changed in the last 40 years that is directly related to the expansion
of economic thinking since the 1960s and with the emergence of the
factory of society, as Mario Tronti so poignantly has described it. I think
this is also why I started our conversation with the question about your
drawings. I think the change in the architectural practice is perfectly
visible in the way some architects draw nowadays. In an abbreviated
form I would argue that the relevant and significant architects drawings
are no longer about how a construction can become a representation
for a situation, but about performance.

Having done the research about the historic moment that I have
just mentioned, it becomes obvious how the practice of architecture is
changing radically. In the late 1960s and early 1970s the old paradigm
of Fordism was still visible, but the new economic paradigm of Post-
Fordism with its new labour conditions would become dominant in
our Western industrial societies that affected the architects and their
practice. She or he need to become performative subjects, as does
their architecture. A good example is Hans Hollein and his Mobile-
Office project. One knows the Mobile Office by Hollein as a kind of
installation. At least in the collection of the Generali Foundation in
Vienna it is archived as an installation as follows: pvc-foil, pneumatic,
electric blower (or vacuum cleaner), typewriter (Hermes Baby),
telephone, drawing board, pencil, rubber, thumbtacks, floor piece
synthetic turf 225 x ø 120 cm. Yet actually it was a performance that

Hollein did for the Austrian Television. It was 30 minute longer portrait about the young architect in which the 1 Minute and 6 Seconds Mobile Office performance is aired. In the portrait Hollein is certainly an entrepreneurial self (a term that was coined by the German sociologist Ulrich Bröckling). He sells himself as the "Idea Man", the global acting architect. Today it might sound like the stereotypical architect's role-model, who has a professorship in Düsseldorf, a building site in New York City and his office still in Vienna. Yet back then it was a radical change in the public appearance of the architect. But it is also the status of the "drawing" and the represented architectural "object" that changes. A video suddenly can be understood to be the "drawing". And the object itself is a transparent pneu. In its concept it is a bubble that has globally standardized circuit points in order to be connected to the world-wide information infrastructure, yet it can adapt to each and every situation, taking on different colours and gives shelter to the global and nomadic labourer.

So it is of course NOT the question for the architect, for the designer or any other contemporary labourer or subject for that matter, either to be an agent of a dominant discourse, or to introduce a radical new order or organization. The latter would dangerously overrate the role of the architect. The architectural practice, or the design practice is somehow both. The question then is rather how one would contribute and change things by affirming a given situation. I call this a "double affirmation". Yet there might also be a situation in which one would need to interrupt the cybernetic control circuit, by refusing a given task. You are completely right to say with Slavoj Žižek that this act of refusal is already part of todays economy. With the repetition of the Bed-In performance by John Lennon and Yoko Ono in Montreal I actually wanted to make another point, that might be crucial for a contemporary practice: with the repetition the performance gets a different rhythm and a different organization. So even though the spatial adaption of the Hilton hotels look the same (white sheets, big window, same slogans, etc), the performance is fundamentally different: in the first instance it is an open, unscripted happening, that has aspects of Yoko Ono's art practice, but also John Lennon's experience as pop-musician. In this very moment, through the affirmation of media, and their own exposure to media, they create a "design" or a "performative space" that actually introduces a different social order. One aspect: Yoko Ono is on par with her husband. Yet in Montreal, the roles get scripted by the Canadian broadcasting corporation with invited guests and clearly assigned roles: John Lennon the hero, Yoko Ono his wife adoring the hero but completely silenced and then a whole bunch of guests with assigned roles. I think one can learn from this that, in order to elude the current logic of capital and its economy, one has to be very flexible. Every repetition is already part of the system. In that sense, maybe we also need to understand your example of the occupied park in Athens Exarcheia area as an already "standardized" and tested format of protest, that is actually not producing the difference that the people involved in it hope for.

AA   Thank you for this clarification, Andreas. Nevertheless I have to add something concerning the underestimation of normality on which all the western modernism tradition is founded. If the problem becomes evident with a repetition, something may be wrong with the repeated principle. I believe it is time to face the consequences of the past; only acting against systems is not enough any more. I cannot support an idealization of events that prioritize the exception and demonize the norm.

AR   I have to fully agree with you in this point!

AA   Then we will both disappoint Badiou here. We need different norms in order to deconstruct the old ones. Even if we simply want to work against the existing order of things, we need small systems to contradict bigger ones. In this sense we are never out of a normalizing action even if we are against a routine; there is a problem concerning our practice there; we work in order to dismantle systems or to act against them without investing on some alternative regulations for different normalities. My strategy seeks possible normalities to inhabit a differently shared infrastructure. New rules for different cohabitations.

Alternative regulating structures may be more dangerous for a status quo than exceptions and idealized events that explode against structures. This confrontation with the system is more and more included in the system. Many struggles and sacrifices were easily incorporated in the normal routine of the nowadays function of the financial world. I try to explore this difficult question of an interesting deregulation that will have the form of an again scripted but different normality. I think of urban protocols as systems of rules that could expand, be projected to more areas, be applied to other parts of the city. Application, testing and expansion would be a dream for instituted new urban protocols. In this sense repetition in my case is something I wish. The specificity of each repetition may disappoint or fulfil the expectations of a protocol. We have here the analogue to a smartphone application projected to the urban fabric; the application can be useful or not; till now I only work to make this need of new urban legislation obvious. I designed for the Lisbon Triennale a transformation of the Syntagma Square to a huge Open Air Office. It could not be operated without a change of the parliament itself! It could not function neither without a different Internet. The regulation for an alternative Internet could change the city quicker than any state bureaucracy. It needs to be consciously legislated to perform a new type of democracy. We will need hackers to collaborate with law specialists for such a project.

I agree that the question is rather how one would change things by affirming a given situation. But let's try to go further than this; how can we use the stereotypical view of the everyday as a starting point? How can we distort this boring and unquestioned normality and produce an uncanny structure? This question leads to the problem of the operating power that could make these projects realistic. Who is introducing this research-like micro legislations that could be tested for a period of time? Can the state give its permission to working teams and institutions to operate legally in a prescribed frame? Can it seriously allow some protocols to be tested for some period of time? My proposed protocol before being adopted poses the question: Who could run an Open Air Office?

Sometimes I am told that such questions are not realistic. I believe the opposite. What I do till now already happens via the Internet or it may happen easily. We miss the consciousness of this process. We know that the market can take command of my Urban Protocols; a lot of indices tell us already that such a thing is getting prepared. But we have to name the exact situation and give a material representation of it, if we do not want this colonization of the public space to happen in a barbaric way. Can we suggest a different normality than the market for these urban devices? Can we think of some hybrid operating systems? This may be the deepest question for architecture nowadays. Who will build the next urban order? I propose my protocols to open the question. We need a technical work to formalize, materialize and represent the question of power today. In the same time to paraphrase Hegel we seek for "the great art of inducing others to be as they are in and for themselves, and to bring this out to the light of consciousness". Urban Protocols are introduced as expendable and repeatable; they can be playtested and declined if we do not need them. There is much danger in the production of "urban apparatuses" or new legislative transformations. They go similar to the production of weapons; we do not know who will use them and for what reason. They can immediately shape power, share the space or offer it to a private company. But if we know how they will look like we may also think about different ways to program them.

Pelin Tan

A   Genealogy

of   Nomadic

Space

"Utopia is not written in the future tense" [1]

How can we read the genealogical link of Antonas's practice both from the 1960s Utopian Urbanism and 1990s self–organized structures of survival practices? How can we understand this practice through a critical spatial thinking? Antonas's projects of nomadic spaces like the KEG *apartment,* the *Crane rooms,* and the plug-in project *Transformable Vertical Village,* are all borrowing from the past genre of Utopist Urbanism, as well as from the alternative practices of dwelling that did rise in the 1990s with references from the Situationist Movement heritage. Although the references and ideas of utopian urbanism and related design proposals of nomad/nomadism, and flexible spaces differs in the beginning of the 20th Century from geographies to movements and cities; either technocratic, formalist utopian urbanism or as criticism towards modernistic urban planning; the possibilities of nomad spaces and flexible grassroots architecture are part of the critical discussions in design.

The criticism of control society and the effect of technology in a negative way on the urban space has been always immanent in the utopian proposals from the scales of dwelling and building, to the city. The desire to propose and design inhabitable spaces, nomad spaces and in-between spaces in architectural and artistic practice have strong roots since the most Western *avant-garde* approaches in the 20th century although they have their own local geographical contexts. However, such approaches and practices not always project in a precise way the future design of living spaces but instead our current existences. As Anthony Vidler expresses about Constant's work: "...*the depiction of inhabitable spaces allowing us to project ourselves into its infinite perspectives, to imagine the realization of the plans. These seem, that its, to make up the concrete specifications for the construction of utopia in the present.*"[2] The degree of its normative form, and the program of the design of utopian spaces is always the triggering point; because of the basic question that is immanence in imagination of utopia. The basic question is *"How can we talk about utopia without integrating the practice of visionary illusion of the revolution?"*, as the Utopie journal asked in 1969. Or in reverse, would utopian design proposals be coherent within the contemporary neoliberal capitalist production around the world, where both housing and dwelling are still basic issues in the 21st century. For the *Utopie* journal, both the approach of urbanists in France in the 1960s, and spatial and visionary urbanism in general, were about normative forms of organizing the society without considering the conflicts and heterogeneity[3]. For the SI movement the drifting subjectivity was in the center of the urban environment, that demanded interventions in the system, based on confusion and decentralized nomadic life.

The claim and approach was totally different than visionary urbanism. For Constant's design, Peter Wollen describes: "a kind of futuristic, inter-urban, aerial *derive*".[4] In this frame Antonas's works *Transformable Vertical Villages*, *Crane Rooms* and KEG *apartments* represent a similar approach. These futuristic, inter-urban and aerial *derive*; open a criticism of a normative utopian proposal and also invites to question the subjectivity within its domestic space (her own shelter). The design of nomadic spaces in the landscape—as mobile structures— and its focus on the apocalyptic subjectivity, marks a different route of utopianism. An utopianism which, goes beyond visionary illusionism and takes an heterogeneous route that indicates the current spatial production in our society.

"You have to think about how to undermine the situation before it undermines you"[5] wrote artist Rirkrit Tiravanija in 1995. Investing, searching about the Utopia now is mostly visible in Tiravanija's practice since the 1990s; coincidentally we should remark that Tiravanija comes from the same generation as Aristide Antonas. Nomadic space is not only a physical entity but also a shared space, a space of future imagined collectivism that has potentialities to appear in the horizon. Nomadism, the flux of the object of the art form, molecular everyday interventions and translocal dwellings are the approaches of situations. Furthermore, another primary reference of nomadic dwelling is Krzysztof Wodiczko's *The Homeless Vehicle Project* designed for—and in collaboration with— homelessness people in New York, in 1987-89.[6] For Wodiczko, being a "refugee" in urban space is a primary archetype of an individual that is searching for the right of dwelling and participation in urban life. Homelessness, refugee, gypsy, nomad... such biopolitical subjectivities among urban production are conditions of survival, inclusion or exclusion of urban life, and artifacts of undermining the living habitat system. Currently, in 21st century, dwelling rights is one of the main and most necessary debates in our cities as well as in disappearing rural life. Neoliberal urban policies of states that are basically joint ventures of both private interests and governmental administration; are harshly effecting and forming our main infrastructures. These policies that are taken under norms of exception are being justified through artificial conceptualization of earthquake, terrorism, security or illegal migration flow. It is possible that a state where the proposal of utopian dwelling structure has strong references from the 20th century, but now it's totally based on different fundamental heterogeneous social and class coexistences. Gated communities in Cape Town, billions of mass housing in China, state-led gentrification in Istanbul, privatization policy of seashores in Greece, endless housing debts in Madrid; are just some of the main examples of the same contradiction and phenomena that evidence the collaboration between state and private interest, that

are continuously producing the artificial imagination of dwelling and urban/rural space.

Reading KEG *apartment* in this context reveals two levels of discussion: A nomadism that is beyond the property rights that fundamentally releases the claim of the right of shelter; secondly the mobility, a gypsy subjectivity that transforms any moving condition into nomadism, the space of a kind of deterritorialization. Thus, both spatial conditions open up the question about what is a nomad space within a larger utopian legacy, that find itself in constraints with our current spatial production. The *Transformable Vertical Village* can be understand as a response to current living systems, as is based in a plug-in approach, following Archigram's Plug-in City, is a self-assembly project where the units that form the ensemble can change place; the whole complex is based on a dismountable and expandable 3D grid which allows the insertion of ship containers or other KEG-like units, giving to the project the flexibility and usability demanded by the growing needs of housing spaces in the city. *Crane rooms* represent a post-apocalyptic solution of dwelling if we consider the housing and shelter urgency as our current catastrophe. Warfare, ecological disaster and technological collapse have deep impacts in our everyday life and in our future. The outcome of warfare is the evicted inhabitants and new constructed city-camps. Ecological disasters are the core reasons for governments to create policies of further demolishment of ecological landscape and its inhabitants. This phase of Anthropocene leads to co-production of governmental and other actors in order to increase the control over the ecological landscape. The technological collapse that appears in drone realities in where non-human pixel driven leads to catastrophes of demolishment of cities and habitats. Eventually, the possibility of the *Crane Rooms* appearing in the future, reminds us our current realities.

The poster-pamphlet UTOPIA E/O RIVOLUZIONE [7] from 1969, reveals still contemporary in our architecture and design related utopian practices: How can we talk about utopia without integrating the practice of visionary illusion of the revolution? I would like to add to this inquiry, how the dialectic of this questioning differs in our contemporary time of trans-local geographical practice, in which all affect and coproduce the spatial reality? I think, Antonas's visionary utopian nomad projects critically reveal current layers of spatial production, and they make this in a subtle way, inviting us to face with each level of reality of spatial production lead by warfare, realities of Anthropocene and dwelling policies nowadays.

1   "Utopia Is Not Written In The Future Tense" Poster-pamphlet distributed on the occasion of the Congress "UTOPIA E/O RIVOLUZIONE" in Turin, April 25, 26, 27, 1969. P.238 From *Utopie – Texts and Projects, 1967-1978*, Edited by Craig Buckley and Jean-Louis Violeau, p. 238

2   Anthony Vidler, "Diagrams of Utopia" in *The Activist Drawing – Retracing Situationist Architecture from Contant's New Babylon to Beyond*, Edt. C. de Zegher & M.Wigley, The Drawing Center, 2001, New York.

3   "Spatial" or "visionary" urbanism were but another facet of more normative and bureaucratic forms of urbanism; in both cases urbanists were caught in a "vortex," consigned to the project of "[reducing] social complexity to

simple, easily manipulable elements at the level of the 'urban' plan." *Utopie – Texts and Projects, 1967-1978*, Edited by Craig Buckley and Jean-Louis Violeau. p. 14

4   Peter Wollen, New Left Review 8, March-April 2001. http://newleftreview.org/II/8/peter-wollen-situationists-and-architecture

5   p. 22, Sherri Geldin, 1998, Supermarket, Rirkrit Tiravanija, Frank Hyde-Antwi, Buchbindereri Burkhardt AG, migros museum für gegenwartskunst Zürich.

6   *Krzysztof Wodizscko – The Homeless Vehicle Project*, Art Random with David Lurie, 1991, Edited by Kyoichi Tsuzuki, Kyoto Shoin Int. Co.Ltd., Japan.

7   Congress "UTOPIA E/O RIVOLUZIONE" in Turin, April 25, 26, 27, 1969.

Aristide Antonas

The

Bloom's

Room

The Bloom's Room is a project that somehow summarises the five urban protocols that conforms this archipelago; it is basically an investigation on the possibilities of a room that provides the simulation of a flight. A system of fake freedom with no limits of the body possibilities is performed. The Bloom's Room is the exaggeration of the rationale of the Google offices or it can be read as a simple prison where the feeling of freedom is identified to the principle of incarcerating. It replaces the space of labor and/or destruction in a possible future society. Instead of being in front of a mere screen, technically it researches on the new functions of a "naked body cockpit". With this project it's possible to discuss how can we transform this reality to a political condition? How can we think about the Internet as a conscious space for another type of legislations now that both the state and the market withdraw?

All the projects of this Archipelago of Protocols relate the self experience of the internet to a common sphere. Considering that the Internet is what makes us "man of the crowd, man of the masses, mass-man..." —as described by Tiqqun— the connection between all the projects is present in the use of the Internet, which is somehow linked to a certain modern concept of "the power to reside anywhere".

217   The Bloom's Room

221   The Bloom's Room

222   The Bloom's Room

Afterword

by   Ethel Baraona

and

César Reyes

"Every step of real movement is more important than a dozen programmes." – Karl Marx, 1875

Don't get confused, Antonas' protocols are a trap. Written in the way a bureaucrat can understand and thus approve, in reality they are addressed to the inhabitants that refuse to accept the city as a static reality ruled by a set of norms and standards. They contain subversive and simple ideas to manage through unconventional appropriation, the nooks of the city falling out of the control of city managers. Naming them protocols, and using legislative jargon is only a way to make them readable and accepted by bureaucracy. But the series of actions included in those lines give much more space to serendipity and improvisation than to regulation. After reading Antonas' own description of his protocols, you will understand that they depict simple facts that make the projects feasible, as the spontaneous appropriation of empty spaces by the citizens. In that sense they refer to relations and actions actually made by citizens without the need of previous regulations.

The Urban Protocols are meant to introduce legal temporary occupancies of the abandoned city center that will be finally accepted and allegedly controlled by a municipal authority. Its main purpose would be to establish cluster-like micro-legislative constructions with communal functions. Surprisingly, the suggestive architectonic outcomes of Antonas' protocols are driven by the immaterial set of relations described, and can finally trigger spatial urban modifications.

Although the proposition of indeterminate spaces, diagonal commonhold, invisible or parasitic councils seem more a terrain of radical literature rather than planning; it seems that such protocols address different metrics and interactions within the cities, like social trust, which are not under the scrutiny of conventional regulations. The possibility of diagonal ownership, to detach the use of spaces from their property, to set communal councils that could directly revise performance of policies; and other strategies to manage the commons; seems a promissory shift in the way planners can finally engage with social dynamics of urban phenomena. The protocols posed by Aristide Antonas are referring to Athens, but somehow could be extrapolated to most of Western cities, or adapted to other relational urban realities. If broadening conventional metrics, planners and city managers could be able to understand the city under the logics of complex systems, thus leaving space to indeterminacy, in favour of human interactions. Understanding which are those protocols could led to the audacity of letting them open to temporary unruled variations, expecting major changes with few manoeuvers.

Antonas relies on technology to register and process the operative dimension of the protocols. However, as a whole they conceptually confront the technofetichist promises that led to the fiction that the city could be fully designed, registered and manipulated. The repetition of certain segments of legislative-like argot, finally reveal other layers which are useful to navigate the complete urban archipelago. For sure you have been able to see them emerging in the oniric representations of the protocols as projects. Squares open as if forensic dissections, drapery working as building enclosures, slides to move between buildings, or open-space working configurations are only the theatre stages that has just been abandoned by the actors of a tragedy, and are just waiting for the next ones to emerge as humans floating in disturbing positions. Here we have an achievement of philosophical representation of architecture in the age of data driven renders. The projects proposed by Antonas depict the immaterial atmosphere that can be perceived in an inhabited space even you cannot see its occupants, and remind us that the city is mainly a set of relations between people, rather than agglomeration of them within built spaces. And such relations are everything but efficient and they can not be fully subjected to control, because they carry within them a degree of subjectivity. In some aspects Antonas' writing and projects suggest a possible representation of *the Bloom* outlined by Tiqqun[1] in their writings; if the Bloom is nothing more than "pure availability to be affected", pure naked humanity; then we have just witnessed in this book, a systematization to redeem and restitute the weight of the infra-ordinary in our lives, and the meaning of community outside the traditional molds of nation, class and identity. And we remark it: pure naked humanity floating within our cities.

If we are able to overcome the fascination and commodification of urban trends, going from smart big data management platforms, to the do-goodism of 'tactical urbanisms'; perhaps it's possible to think that a new model can emerge from networks of confidence working at neighbourhood scale, on transitional common spaces and activities; to trigger dialogues with the challenges of a society that intends to overcome the myths of the welfare state and the hardships labelled as austerity by capitalism. The system will resist, and we may use some traps in this task.

1   Tiqqun is the name of a French philosophical journal, founded in 1999 with an aim to "recreate the conditions of another community." In extension it refers to the philosophical concept which stems from these texts. According to Michèle Alliot-Marie, the French Interior Minister during Sarkozy's mandate, Tiqqun are 'ultra-leftist-anarchist' subversives, members of an 'invisible committee' plotting the violent downfall of capitalism." And that's enough reference to pay attention to what they are saying.

Archipelago of Protocols
Project's Credits

Shared Terraces
Architect: Aristide Antonas
Collaborator: Katerina Koutsogianni
Architectural Competition,
    First Prize

Roof Playgrounds
Architect: Aristide Antonas
Collaborator: Katerina Koutsogianni

Open Air Office
Architect: Aristide Antonas
Collaborators: Katerina
    Koutsogianni, Kristy Garikou,
    Alexis Georgiadis

Weak Monumental Square
Arhitect: Aristide Antonas
Collaborator: Katerina Koutsogianni

Transformable Vertical Village
Architect: Aristide Antonas
Collaborators: Katerina
    Koutsogianni, Stefanos Filippas

Agglomeration of Empty Shops
Architect: Aristide Antonas
Collaborators: Elina Axioti, Katerina
    Koutsogianni, Katerina
    Grigoropoulou

The Trench and the Arcade
Architect: Aristide Antonas
Collaborators: Katerina
    Koutsogianni, Platon Issaias

Urban Hall
Architect: Aristide Antonas
Civil Engineer: Christos Kaklamanis
Consultant: Aris Tsagrasoulis
Collaborators: Katerina
    Koutsogianni, Kristy Garikou

Bloom's Room
Architect: Aristide Antonas
Collaborators: Katerina
    Koutsogianni

Aristide Antonas Greek architect and writer with a PhD in Philosophy, a professor of Architecture Design and Theory, director of the post graduate program at the University of Thessaly, post graduate seminar director in the National Technical University of Athens and the owner of the Antonas office. Co-curator for the Greek Pavilion, Venice Biennale 2004, co-founder of the plural academic persona "Gregorios Pharmakis", co-founder of Built Event, (spatial practices for architecture, art, curating and urbanism, presented in Barcelona Landscape Biennale 2006, Sao Paulo Biennale of Architecture 2007, Galleria Contemporaneo, Mestre, Italy, 2008, Thessaloniki Biennale 2009 and Gyoumri Biennale Armenia, 2010). Writer of 6 literature books in Greece, 2 published theater scripts and plays performed in Greece, France and Germany, essays published on various sites on the Internet. He designed vacation houses and presented non commissioned research architecture; his ebook Murder Fact Event was published by dpr barcelona in 2015 and a monography about his houses was published in Italy by Luca Galofaro; Aristide Antonas, Libra 2015. The Antonas office was nominee for a Mies Van der Rohe award in 2009, for a Iakov Chernikov Prize in 2011 and had the archmarathon first prize for the Open Air Office in Beirut in 2015.

Athena Athanasiou teaches at Panteion University of Social and Political Sciences, in Athens, Greece. She has authored the books: *Life at the Limit: Essays on Gender, Body and Biopolitics* (Athens, 2007); *Crisis as a State of Exception: Critiques and Resistances* (Athens, 2012); and she has co-authored (with Judith Butler) *Dispossession: The Performative in the Political* (Polity Press, 2013). She has also edited the volumes: *Feminist Theory and Cultural Critique* (Athens, 2006); *Rewriting Difference: Luce Irigaray and 'the Greeks'* (co-ed. with Elena Tzelepis, SUNY Press, 2010); and *Biosocialities* (Athens, 2011). Her new book *Unthinkable Mourning: Counter-Memory and Feminist Political Subjectivity in Post-Yugoslavia* will be published by Edinburgh University Press. She is a fellow at the Center for the Study of Social Difference, at Columbia University, and vice president of the Nicos Poulantzas Institute, Athens.

Keller Easterling is an architect, writer and professor at Yale. Her most recent book, *Extrastatecraft: The Power of Infrastructure Space* (Verso, 2014), examines global infrastructure networks as a medium of polity. Another recent book, *Subtraction* (Sternberg, 2014), considers building removal or how to put the development machine into reverse.

Other books include: *Enduring Innocence: Global Architecture and its Political Masquerades* (MIT, 2005) and *Organization Space: Landscapes, Highways and Houses in America* (MIT, 1999).

Andreas Rumpfhuber is a registered Architect and Theoretician. With his office Expanded Design he works on urban design and architecture projects in Vienna, Austria, as well on international Reseach Projects. The main focus of the work are spaces for work and (public) housing. He currently is Guest Professor for Urban Design at the Academy of Fine Arts in Stuttgart, Germany. His books include: *Architektur immaterieller Arbeit* (2013), *The Design of Scarcity* (Strelka Press, 2014) and *Modelling Vienna. Real Fictions in Social Housing* (Turia + Kant, 2015)

Pelin Tan is a sociologist and art historian. She concluded her PhD on socially engaged art in urban space and her post-doc on methodology of artistic research at MIT. Tan researched artist run spaces and urban justice in Europe (2004), Asia and Japan (2012, 2015). With Anton Vidokle, she is the co-director of sci-fi film episodes 2084 about the future of art. She is a member of video collectives Artıkişler/videoccupy and bak.ma an open digital media archive

of political movements in Turkey. Sociologist/Art Historian, Associate Professor, Architecture Faculty, Mardin Artuklu University, Turkey. Guest Research Associate Professor in Hong Kong Polytechnic, Design MA Program (2016, Spring). Lead author of *Toward new Urban Society* chapter of *IPSP* (Edt.S.Sassen&E. Peterse, 2017).

Dr. Thanos Zartaloudis is an academic teaching and researching at Kent Law School, University of Kent and at the Architectural Association, School of Architecture, London, UK. His background is in law, philosophy and architectural theory and history. He is the editor of a book series with Edinburgh University Press titled *Encounters in Law and Philosophy*. His most recent book is *Giorgio Agamben: Power, Law and the Uses of Criticism* (Routledge, 2011). His forthcoming books include: *The Use of Things* (2017) and *The Idea of Justice* (EUP, 2016). He has recently completed his first novel titled *The Searchers of the City* (to be published in Greek in 2016).

Archipelago of Protocols
  Aristide Antonas

First Edition dpr-barcelona, 2016

Editors: Ethel Baraona Pohl,
  Cesar Reyes Nájera

Design by Numa/Merino

Contributors: Thanos Zartaloudis,
  Athena Athanasiou, Andreas
  Rumpfhuber, Pelin Tan, and
  Keller Easterling

ISBN: 978-84-942414-2-0
D.L. B 9525-2016

Printed in Barcelona by Agpograf

dpr-barcelona
  Viladomat 59, 4-4
  08015 Barcelona, Spain
  T +34 931 623 528

www.dpr-barcelona.com
twitter: @dpr_barcelona

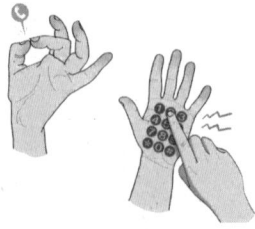